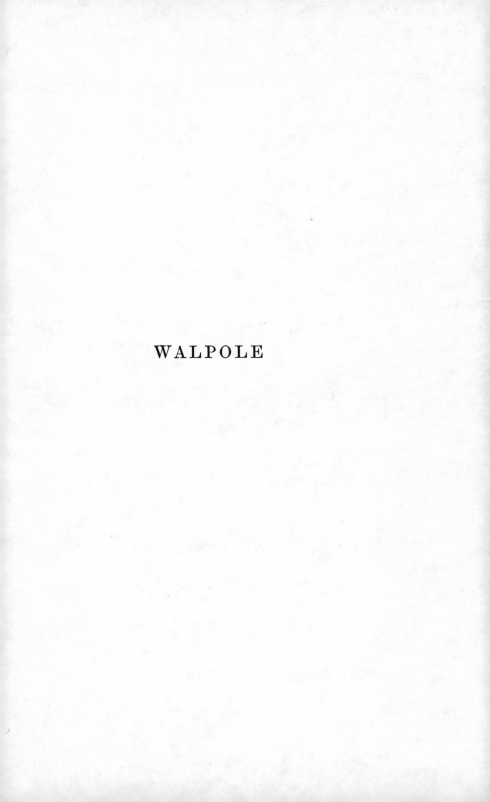

WALPOLE

WALPOLE

BY

JOHN MORLEY

GREENWOOD PRESS, PUBLISHERS
WESTPORT, CONNECTICUT

Originally published in 1889
by Macmillan and Company, London and New York

First Greenwood Reprinting 1971

Library of Congress Catalogue Card Number 76-110858

SBN 8371-4527-9

Printed in the United States of America

CONTENTS

CHAPTER VII

CHAPTER VIII

CHAPTER IX

CHAPTER X

CHAPTER XI

CHAPTER I

WALPOLE was born in August 1676. He came fifth among nineteen children born to Mr. Robert Walpole, a country gentleman of Norfolk, of good estate and ancient lineage. The founder of the family had come over with William of Normandy, and the stock had shown its vigour by an unbroken descent in the male line for no fewer than eighteen generations. Walpoles had been knights of the shire as far back as Edward II. Edward Walpole, grandfather of the future minister, sat in the Convention Parliament of 1660. He is said to have acquired a respectable character for eloquence and weight; he voted for the restoration of Charles II, and he was made a Knight of the Bath. Robert, his son, was in Parliament from the Revolution until his death in 1700. An active Whig in politics, he was a man of marked prudence and credit in his private conduct. A good name in those days was not incompatible with a jovial temper and much steady drinking. Mr. Walpole was fond of sport, fond of farming and business, and fond of plenty of company and plenty of Nottingham ale. He always took care of his money. An old book, in which he set down all his expenses, showed that he knew how to live in London for upwards of three months for the moderate sum of sixty-five pounds seven shillings and fivepence.

Mr. Walpole sent his third son to Eton and to King's College at Cambridge, not because he valued education, even if education could now have been obtained in those famous foundations, but because he designed the young man to push his fortunes in the Church, then the usual field for a cadet of decent family. But the youth had higher destinies before him than fat livings and an easy bishopric. His elder brother died in 1698, and Robert the younger, becoming heir to the family estates, quitted the university, and settled down with his convivial father to learn all that pertains to the management of land and the enjoyment of country life. It is said that Robert the elder used to insist on making his son drink more than his just share, on the ground that no son should ever be allowed to have enough of his senses to see that his father was tipsy. Amid such surroundings, which, though compared with the more polished surface of modern manners they seem coarse and rough, yet were vigorous, hearty, and practical, Walpole reached his twenty-fourth year. His father vowed that he would make him the first grazier in the country. Higher destinies were in store for him. The young squire, under a homely exterior, covered a powerful understanding, a strong will, a good eye for men, and a union of solid judgment with commanding ambition, which fitted him to rule a kingdom, and to take his place among the foremost men in Europe.

In the summer of 1700 he married Miss Catherine

Shorter, a daughter of Sir John Shorter, then Lord
Mayor of London. The lady brought him beauty, good
manners, and a fortune. Before the end of the year
his father died at the early age of fifty, and Robert
Walpole came into the estate. Nearly the whole of
it lay in the county of Norfolk, and as it was then let,
the rent-roll amounted to something over two thousand
pounds a year. The property carried with it a couple of
pocket boroughs, Castle Rising and Lynn. Mr. Walpole
was at once (January 1701) elected for the first of them,
rendered vacant by his father's decease, and he retained
the seat until the death of King William. In 1702, on
the accession of Queen Anne, he was returned for Lynn
Regis; he continued to sit for the same borough without
interruption until his fall from power forty years later.
It is sometimes said that the advance of democracy has
destroyed this stability of relation between representatives and constituents; but it is worth noting that two
members of the existing House of Commons (1889) have
held what are virtually the same seats without a break,
one of them for fifty-nine years, and the other for fifty-
four.

The moment of Walpole's entrance upon parliamentary
life was one of critical importance in national history.
The great question which had been opened and provi-
sionally closed by the events of 1688, was whether the
English monarchy should be limited and Protestant, or
absolute, Catholic, and dependent on France. The work
of the Revolution may seem at this distance of time to
have been out of danger by the beginning of the
eighteenth century. Even if it were true that the bulk
of the nation had made up its mind, this is not always a

guarantee against surprise and against accident, as an
incident of our own generation may serve to show.
France in 1873 had made up its mind for a Republic,
yet only a personal caprice, or stubborn principle, in the
Comte de Chambord saved France from a legitimist
restoration. The calamity of a legitimist restoration
in England was only avoided by the sagacity and the
resolution, first of the king, and then of the Whig leaders.

Walpole joined the Whigs in supporting the Act
of Settlement, but he is not known to have taken
part in debate. Personal emulation is stated to have
been the spur that first made him a speaker. At Eton
he had been the schoolfellow, if not the rival of a lad
who was destined to one of the most singular careers in
political history. St. John, better known by his
later title of Bolingbroke, was two years younger than
Walpole, and he entered Parliament about the same
time. He had not been many months in the House of
Commons before gifts of incomparable brilliancy brought
him to the very front place among the debaters of his
time. The occasion of Walpole's maiden speech is not
known. All that is told is that he was confused and
embarrassed, and failed to realise the expectations of his
friends. He was followed by somebody more fluent
than himself. "You may applaud the one," said an
acute onlooker, "and ridicule the other, as much as you
please; but depend upon it, the spruce gentleman who
made the set speech will never improve, and Walpole
will in time become an excellent speaker." Walpole
took pains to fulfil the prediction by relying on his
native qualities; he was active in business, attentive to
all that went on, keen in observing men and watching

opportunity, and staunch to the principles and the party that he had adopted for his own.

Walpole was first introduced into government,—that important moment in the life of a member of Parliament —in a subordinate post on the council of Prince George of Denmark. The appointment was made on the recommendation of no less important a personage than Marlborough. The prince was the queen's husband, and because he was the husband of the queen, he had been made Lord High Admiral of England. The naval board had provoked bitter complaints of mismanagement, negligence, and corruption, and the leading Whigs, not yet fully reconciled with the administration of Marlborough and Godolphin, whose transformation was still incomplete, actively echoed the outcry of the merchants against the Lord High Admiral and his advisers. Walpole said the best that could be said for his colleagues, and when he was reproached with the terrible sin of speaking against some of his own party, he answered with spirit that he would never be so mean as to sit at a board and not defend it. At the same time, as he had to defend the board, he did his best to improve it. In this inferior office he first showed those qualities of a great man of business which, along with his extraordinary general power of mind and character, afterwards made him a great minister. Godolphin, then the head of the government, was himself a man of business just short of the very first class. The contemporary authorities tell us that Walpole won his chief's admiration by his energy and punctuality in affairs, his precision in accounts, his insight into finance, and his easy manners. In a short time he was called upon to exhibit these qualifications in a more important field.

The first Parliament of Anne was strongly Tory. The House of Lords, numbering before the Union with Scotland about one hundred and ninety members, including the bishops and the Catholic peers who could not sit, contained the representatives of the great families who had made and guided the Revolution of 1688. Here, therefore, the Whigs held a uniform predominance. But they had no share in the leading posts of administration for three years after the accession of the queen. Marlborough and Godolphin were the two heads of Anne's first government, and they remained so until the great ministerial revolution in 1710. During this period of eight years the government passed through no fewer than three important changes. First Marlborough and Godolphin were joined by the high Tories, with the Earl of Nottingham at their head. Then in 1704 the high Tories were displaced, and Godolphin took in the more moderate and, we must add, the more unprincipled section of the same party, in the persons of Harley and St. John. They were brought in as the particular friends of Marlborough, and were meant by him to balance the Whig influence of Cowper and Sunderland. It was to be not government by parties, but government by groups. Finally, the General and the Treasurer, as the two leaders were called, found themselves slowly driven to look in the Whig direction, and in 1706 they pressed the Earl of Sunderland into the government, against the vehement wishes of the queen, and to the great displeasure of their colleagues. Halifax told them they were mixing oil with vinegar.

The uneasy combination lasted until the beginning of 1708. It then fell to pieces, and government by groups came necessarily to an end. Harley's furtive ambitions, spurred on by the restless and intrepid St. John, made any subordinate position privately irksome to him. He began, in Bishop Burnet's phrase, to set up for himself, and to act no more under the direction of the Lord Treasurer. Where anything was to be got, said his bitterest enemy in later years, Harley always knew how to wriggle himself in; when any misfortune threatened, he knew how to wriggle himself out. A bedchamber revolution helped him. The Treasurer and the General soon discovered Harley's practices; they went to the queen, and finding her unwilling to part with him, declared themselves bound to quit her service. The scene that followed is a curious example of the difference in ministerial procedure between that time and our own. The day was Sunday, and a Cabinet council had already been summoned. The queen in those days sat at their meetings, just as she systematically attended on all important discussions in the House of Lords, and was even upon one occasion personally appealed to by Marlborough in the course of the debate in that chamber. After Marlborough and Godolphin had left the presence, Anne immediately went to the Cabinet council. "Harley," says Burnet, "opened some matters relating to foreign affairs: the whole board was very uneasy; the Duke of Somerset said he did not see how they could deliberate on such matters, since the General was not with them; he repeated this with some vehemence, while all the rest looked so cold and sullen that the Cabinet council was soon at an end;

and the queen saw that the rest of her ministers and chief officers were resolved to withdraw from her service if she did not recall the two that had left it." It was said, the writer goes on to tell us, that she was ready to put all to the hazard, but the caution and timidity of Harley prevented her. She sent for Marlborough the next day, and after some expostulations told him that Harley would go. Anne's resentment was deep, and though she was obliged to take the two leaders back into her service, they never recovered either her favour or her confidence. The important fact during the first eight years of the reign of Queen Anne is not that the administration was first Tory, then composite of Whig and Tory, and in its final stage pure Whig, but that it was in all its stages, whether Whig or Tory, a Marlborough administration, seconding the policy, providing means for the projects, and devoted to the person of that great and powerful genius.

This was the most important of the three changes that preceded the great party revolution of the last four years of the reign. It brought about that government by a particular political connection which Burke some sixty years later singled out as the grand illustration, furnished by one of the most fortunate periods in our history, of the virtue of Party. "These wise men," he said, "for such I must call Lord Sunderland, Lord Godolphin, Lord Somers, and Lord Marlborough, were too well principled in those maxims upon which the whole fabric of public strength is built, to be blown off their ground by the breath of every childish talker. They were not afraid that they should be called an ambitious junto; or that their resolution to stand or fall together should, by placemen, be interpreted into a scuffle for places." Godolphin now for the first time formed his government on a basis exclusively Whig. It was on this occasion, in the spring of 1708, that Walpole was made Secretary for War in the room of St. John.

The Lord Treasurer was far from being a mere figure-head. Godolphin was one of the men of a type that a great revolution seldom fails to throw up—silent, able, pliant, assiduous, indispensable. He was the younger son of a Cornish gentleman. The Godolphins made their first appearance in public life in the latter half of the six-teenth century, and the fortunes and influence of their house grew so rapidly that throughout the seventeenth century their only rivals in Cornwall were the Grenvilles.[1] It was to the head of the house of Godophin, as his most honoured friend, that Hobbes dedicated the *Leviathan*. His son, Sidney, is described by Clarendon as a young gentleman of incomparable parts, who being of delicate education and constitution, and unacquainted with con-tentions, upon his observation in the House of Commons of the wickedness of the king's enemies, out of the pure indignation of his soul and conscience to his country, engaged himself with the royalists. The Sidney Go-dolphin of Queen Anne was of less delicate mould. He began his career as a page in the household of Charles II, and at the same time, oddly enough, he had, like Harley, entered the House of Commons as member for one of the forty-two parliamentary constituencies which Corn-

---

[1] See p. 45 of Mr. W. Prideaux Courtney's *Parliamentary Repre-sentation of Cornwall to* 1832—an excellent piece of work, of especial interest in connection with Walpole, who owed so much to Cornish boroughs.

wall at that time possessed. From 1626 to 1766 a
Godolphin had been returned thirty-seven times for
Helston, and with a very brief interruption the minister
held the seat until his elevation to the peerage. Charles
used to say of him, that Sidney Godolphin was never
in the way and never out of the way. He guarded the
public treasury with the jealous watchfulness of a miser
over his hoard. He resisted a job, even when it was
backed by the mighty influence of Marlborough, and
when he sanctioned a warrant for the supply of a new
silver trumpet for a troop of the Guards, he minuted
it with an inquiry what had become of the old one.
All governments were equally indifferent to him, and he
took care not to make himself impossible either at
Kensington or St. Germains. Before the death of
Charles II, Godolphin had risen to be a peer and
First Commissioner of the Treasury. James II made
him chamberlain to the queen, and he was often
bitterly reproached in after years for the exuberant
complacency with which he had attended his royal
mistress to her papistical devotions. After William
of Orange had landed, and James was about to leave
Whitehall, Godolphin was one of the five Lords whom
he left to represent him in his absence. This did not
prevent him from immediately acquiring in turn the
confidence of King William, or from resuming his post
at the Treasury, the one Tory in a Whig administration.
Then for a while he withdrew, but before long he was
again First Commissioner, and while he was thus the
trusted servant of William, he secretly took pains to send
messages to James at St. Germains that no kindness
from the usurper could ever make him forget his duty

to his lawful king. This was the shiftiness of the times.
It did not prevent Pope from praising Patritio's hand
unstained, his uncorrupted heart, his comprehensive head
(*Moral Essays*, i. 80). By a strange paradox, the most
solid and precise financier of his day was one of the most
inveterate gamesters : "His pride was in piquet, New-
market fame, and judgment at a bet." It delivered him,
he said, from the necessity of talking. Godolphin was
at least free from the vice of personal rapacity. His
probity at the Exchequer was absolutely unstained.
When he died, after more than five and twenty years
of nearly continuous public employment, he left no
larger sum behind him than twelve thousand pounds.
It has been justly contended on his behalf that a
financier who could year after year raise the vast
sums that were required for Marlborough's great campaigns without public disturbance, and without serious
detriment to the national credit, must have been a
minister of extraordinary skill, capacity, and resource.

Besides this strong testimony to his ability, Godolphin's
ministry will always be remembered in connection with
one domestic event of the highest degree of political
importance : I mean the incorporating union between
England and Scotland. This was a transaction that
abounded in delicate issues. Many sober judges
despaired of ever seeing the consummation of so
momentous a treaty. Those who were most sanguine
expected the negotiations to be protracted for several
years. With an expedition that was of happy omen,
the matter was begun and closed within the compass of
a single year. Brilliant as was the lustre, and real as
was the importance of Blenheim and Ramillies, Ouden-

arde and Malplaquet, those glorious days were infinitely less fruitful in fortunate consequences to the realm than the 6th day of March 1707, when Queen Anne went down to the House of Lords and gave the royal assent to the Act approving and ratifying the Treaty of Union between the two kingdoms henceforth to be known as Great Britain.

The immediate consequences of the measure were not favourable to the ministers who carried it. The Union involved the admission of Presbyterians to Parliament, and this strengthened the cry, which was so loud during the first fifteen years of the century, that the Church was in danger. The exclusion of Harley, St. John, and the Tories from government had sent the Church over into violent opposition. The disappearance of the measure against Occasional Conformity heightened the alarm, and an Act (1709) for nationalising all foreign Protestants who had settled in England, was full of offence to the inflamed partisans of a national Establishment. At the general election of 1705 the clergy and the universities had spread over the country tragic apprehensions of the danger of the Church, but Marlborough's victories were an irresistible argument on the other side. In the general election three years later,—for the reader will not forget that this was the time of triennial Parliaments,—the drum ecclesiastic had again been beaten, with no better result to the High Churchmen in Parliament. A reaction was near at hand, and prudent observers like Walpole may well have foreseen it.

The tide was undoubtedly setting against the Whigs. But in politics the occasion is everything. The general current of the time may be for a government or against

a government, yet the breaking of the wave often
depends upon some small incidental thing done or left
undone. Godolphin gratuitously furnished his antagon-
ists with the occasion that was wanted, and the great
crisis came rapidly to a head in a wholly unexpected
form. In disturbed times an important feature is the
calendar of political fasts and festivals. The com-
memoration of anniversaries has always marked dangerous moments in the last hundred years of French
government, and on a humbler scale in the annals of
Ireland since the Union. The political saints'-days in
England in the reign of Anne were the 30th January,
the date of the martyrdom of the blessed King Charles
I; the 29th May, the birthday and the day of the
restoration of his blessed son, King Charles II; and the
5th November, the day on which, in 1605, the king and
the three estates of the realm had their wonderful
escape from the most traitorous and bloodily-intended
massacre by gunpowder,—and the day on which also,
by a striking coincidence, William of Orange had
landed at Torbay eighty-three years later for the
deliverance of our Church and nation. Sermons on
these famous dates now, and for many years to come,
gave an opportunity too good to be lost for talking
violent politics. A sermon at St. Paul's was like a
modern demonstration in Hyde Park, and the great controversy between Hoadley, of St. Peter-le-Poer, and
Blackhall, of St. Mary Aldermary, excited the same kind
of interest as Newport programmes and Midlothian
manifestoes. Dr. Price's discourse at the dissenting
meeting-house in the Old Jewry on 4th November 1789
laid the train for Burke's *Reflections on the French Revolu-*

tion. It was Dr. Sacheverell's sermon on November 5th, 1709, that provoked the most violent Tory explosion of the century. Sacheverell was a clergyman of respectable family, a fellow of Magdalen College, Oxford, and rector of St. Saviour's Church, Southwark. He possessed no marked ability, but he had some of the gifts of the pulpit, and was a popular city preacher on the Tory side. Addison had been his contemporary and friend at Magdalen, and is supposed to have dedicated one of his early poems to him. In a sermon in 1702 he had boasted that he hung out "a bloody flag and banner of defiance" against all dissenters, and the pleasant phrase gave lively satisfaction to his friends. His historic discourse at St. Paul's on November 5th, 1709, is vehement, heated, and uncompromising, and it contains much strong language about dissenters, and the false brethren who connived at dissent; but it hardly deserves to be dismissed as absurd and scurrilous. It was a bold declaration, without qualification or exception, of the general principle of passive obedience and non-resistance to government, with practical inuendoes that pointed unmistakably against the whole revolution settlement. The Lord Mayor, who was among the congregation at St. Paul's, and who was a Tory member of Parliament, thanked the preacher for his sermon, took him home to dinner, urged him to publish it, and accepted the dedication. Forty thousand copies found buyers.

The government felt that this was an attack on the existing order that could not be passed over. Marlborough, Somers, and Walpole inclined to the view that it might be left to an ordinary prosecution at law. Godolphin, however, stung by a nickname cast upon him by Sacheverell, supported the violent and impetuous Sunderland in urging impeachment; and this course was resolved upon. As events turned out, the decision was disastrous to the government and to the Whig party. The error was not wholly without excuse. The great constitutional battle was not yet secure, and if Sacheverell's sermon meant anything, it meant condemnation of the principles of the Revolution, of the settlement of the Crown, and of the Act and the policy of Toleration. Historians, looking merely to the result, are for the most part of opinion that the impeachment was impolitic and a blunder. Burke, on the contrary, in whose political circle all the circumstances of the fall of the Whigs in 1710 must have remained as a living tradition, seems to approve of the impeachment. It seldom happens to a party, he says in a familiar passage of the *Appeal from the New to the Old Whigs*, to have the opportunity of a clear, authentic, recorded declaration of their political tenets upon the subject of a great constitutional event. The Whigs made that opportunity. "The impeachment of Dr. Sacheverell was undertaken by a Whig ministry and a Whig House of Commons, and carried on before a prevalent and steady majority of Whig peers. It was carried on for the express purpose of stating the true grounds and principles of the Revolution. It was carried on for the purpose of condensing the principles on which the Revolution was first opposed and afterwards calumniated, in order by a juridical sentence of the highest authority to confirm and fix Whig principles, as they had operated both in the resistance to King James, and in the subsequent settlement, and to fix them in the extent and with the limitations with which it was meant that they should be understood by posterity."

Walpole was appointed to be one of the managers for the impeachment, and though he had not favoured the step in council, he was its most energetic agent in the House of Commons. His arguments and those of his colleagues on one side, taken along with those of Sir Simon Harcourt and Bishop Atterbury on the other side (if Atterbury was the author of the Doctor's speech in his own defence), are a complete and satisfactory presentation of the two party positions.

The commotion itself has been so often described that it is unnecessary to tell over again here how Sacheverell became the hero of the hour; how each day during the three weeks of his trial he was attended by an immense crowd of zealous admirers rending the air with their huzzas, and struggling to kiss his hand as he went from his lodging in the Temple along the Strand to Westminster Hall; how his effigies were sold in every street; how his health was drunk before the queen's, and in the same glass with that of the Church; how the London mob attacked meeting-houses, burned the pews and furniture, and maltreated all who would not shout as they did; and how they pressed round the queen herself in her sedan chair at the door of Westminster Hall, crying, "God bless your majesty and the Church, we hope your majesty is for Dr. Sacheverell." He was as popular in the provinces as in the capital; his journey through the midlands to a living in Shropshire was like a royal progress; and the booksellers sold more copies of his trial than of anything since Dryden's *Absalom and Achitophel.* The final sentence was lenient enough to

satisfy even the half - contemptuous indulgence of
modern days.   When the trial was over, the Lords
decreed that he should be suspended from preaching for
three years, and that his sermon should be publicly
burnt, along with some other obnoxious matters and
things, in the presence of the Lord Mayor and the
Sheriffs of London.

Walpole published a pamphlet in the shape of
four letters on this whole transaction, when all was
over; proving "in clear and familiar language, and
by a plain but strong deduction of reasoning, that
the abettors of Sacheverell were the abettors of the
Pretender; and that those who agreed with him to
condemn such resistance as dethroned the father, could
have no other meaning than the restoration of the son."
What was much more important was the practical moral
that was drawn by Walpole for his own use.   It gave
him an aversion and horror at any interposition in the
affairs of the Church, and led him to assume occasionally
a line of conduct which appeared even to militate against
those principles of general toleration to which he was
naturally and by creed inclined.

CHAPTER II

EMBOLDENED by this extraordinary manifestation of sentiments with which she was privately in such strong sympathy, the queen proceeded to change her ministers with as much eagerness as George III showed in dismissing Mr. Fox on the defeat of his India Bill in 1783. Her new advisers did not at once dare to displace Marlborough from his command, but with that important exception the administration was substantially changed. Harley, at first taking only the office of Chancellor of the Exchequer, was the mainspring of the new government, and was shortly installed as Lord Treasurer. Harcourt was first Lord Keeper and then Lord Chancellor, and Rochester was made President of the Council. The most important of all the appointments was that of St. John as Secretary of State. It is interesting to note that this is the last occasion on which a prelate of the Church was made a member of a government. The Bishop of Bristol became Lord Privy Seal.

The general election of 1710 was conducted with extraordinary violence, especially in the large towns. Boisterous crowds barred the way to the polling booth, and in many places there was open, flagrant, and brutal intimidation.   The clergy placed themselves at the head of the agitation.   They filled their sermons with inflammatory topics; they went about from house to house pressing their flocks to show on this great occasion their zeal for the Church; they assured them that now or never was the time to deliver their queen from the bondage in which her late ministers had kept her.   The result was a great victory for the new men.   When people tell us that our present popular franchise is responsible for what are styled the violent turnover majorities of the last twenty years, it is well to remember that fluctuations at least as remarkable took place on the old system in the exciting and critical decade at the beginning of the last century.   There has never been a more rapid electoral transition than that from the great Whig majority in 1708, to the great Tory majority in 1710. Two hundred and seventy members lost their seats. The installation of the Tory ministry was the first strong attempt to break the Whig chain, the first vigorous effort in the long struggle between the Crown and that party, which did not finally close until the victory of the younger Pitt over Fox in 1784.   Ranke has justly observed that Queen Anne's last administration is what gives her reign its marked character in English history.

One of the first measures in the new Parliament was a vindictive attack, according to the fierce spirit of the time, upon the fallen ministers.   Serious efforts had been made by Harley to induce Walpole to remain. It was not in Harley's designs to make a clean sweep, and the history of the Godolphin administration is enough to show that a clean sweep was not yet the accepted principle of a change of government. The sovereign was still free to man each department of state as she thought fit, without paying more attention than she pleased to the wishes of her chief adviser, or to the relations of a given minister with his colleagues. The collective feeling and principle which is the foundation of the modern Cabinet did not then exist. Harley from the outset looked for Whig aid to protect him against the highfliers among his own allies. He gave it out that "a Whig game was intended at bottom," and made earnest advances to Walpole, telling him that he was as good as half of his party put together. Walpole was too long-headed to accept the flattering invitation. His strong and straightforward mind had already grasped the cardinal truth that it was no longer possible for a mixed and composite government to deal with the immense difficulties of the time, and that only a vigorous, concentrated, and continuous administration could be trusted to bring the country through its dangers. He refused Harley's solicitations, though, by a singular variation from modern official usage, he retained for several months after the Whig ministry had been broken up the place of treasurer of the navy, which he had held along with the office of Secretary for War.

When the majority had opened their great attack on Godolphin's management of the public purse, to the effect that the enormous sum of thirty-five millions sterling was unaccounted for, Walpole published a couple of replies, effectually disposing of the charge against his chief, and securing for himself the character of the best man of figures of his time. He was so successful that his adversaries declared it to be the one thing needful to get him out of the House. The charge against him was that he had corruptly received a thousand pounds in connection with a contract for forage while he was Secretary for War. It was resolved (January 1712) that Mr. Walpole had been guilty of a high breach of trust and notorious corruption, that he should be committed to the Tower, and that he should be expelled from the House and disqualified for re-election during the Parliament. Notwithstanding this resolution the borough of Lynn at once proceeded again to elect him, and he was again expelled, thus furnishing the closest precedent to the more famous constitutional case of Wilkes and the electors of Middlesex sixty years afterwards. Walpole published a strenuous vindication of himself while he lay in the Tower, but it is not satisfactory according to the salutary rigour of modern standards of administrative purity. He had undoubtedly not received a shilling for himself out of the contract, but he had bargained that his friend should receive a share in it, and the contractors had bought out the friend by payment of a thousand pounds. We should all be horrified at such good nature at the public expense in any modern minister, but the fact that Walpole made no personal gain completely exonerated him with his contemporaries.

Upon his release at the close of the session, Walpole was much too keen a party man, and too honestly interested in the great national issues at stake, to be an idle onlooker. He wrote various political pieces, and he magnanimously and cheerfully performed that indefinable and mystic function which is so highly valued by the parliamentary whipper-in, and known as keeping the

party together. The hospitality with which he entertained his political associates, we are told, endeared him
to the party and animated their counsels. A story is
told, that he paid a farewell visit to Godolphin, who lay
dying at one of the houses of the Duchess of Marlborough at St. Albans (1712); and that the old statesman, pointing to Walpole, urged her never to forsake
him, "for if souls are permitted to return to the earth,
I will appear to reproach you for your conduct."

The great achievement of the Tory administration was
the Peace of Utrecht (1713). "I am afraid," says Bolingbroke with cynical frankness, "that we came to court in
the same dispositions as all parties have done; that the
principal spring of our actions was to have the government of the state in our hands; that our principal views
were the conservation of this power, great employments
to ourselves, and great opportunities of rewarding those
who had helped to raise us, and of hurting those who
stood in opposition to us." At the same time he held
that the Peace, though the only solid foundation for a
Tory system, was also a necessity and a blessing both
for the country and for Europe. No transaction in
our annals has ever given rise to more violent and
protracted disputes. It is one of the landmarks of
European history, like the treaties of Munster in the
seventeenth century, of Paris and of Versailles in the
eighteenth, and of Vienna in the nineteenth. It effected
an astonishing aggrandisement of the position of England
in Europe, it made wider room for her polity and her
trade in the New World, and it inflicted sufficient humiliation on her two most powerful rivals in the Old. For
twelve years England, the Empire, and Holland had

carried on war against the House of Bourbon in France and in Spain. Marlborough, as the General-in-Chief of the allies, in face of the extraordinary difficulties inseparable from the management of a confederacy so great, so complex, with such diverse interests, had won year after year a series of mighty victories over the French, which can only be compared to the crushing defeats inflicted on the European monarchies a hundred years later by Napoleon Bonaparte. At the moment when Queen Anne dismissed Godolphin, the great English general had Louis XIV at his mercy. With the fall of the Whigs all was changed. France once more raised her head. The allies heard the news from London with profound dismay. The Dutch exchanged their ordinary phlegm for anger and consternation. But Bolingbroke and Harley did not shrink. The victorious soldier, whose career for so many years had been an unbroken tale of triumph in marches, sieges, battles, and negotiations, was dismissed from his commands, as if he were the worst of public offenders, instead of being the deliverer of Europe and the glory of his country. The deposition of Marlborough was as truly one chief aim in pushing the Peace of Utrecht, as one chief aim in the Peace of Paris fifty years later was the deposition of Pitt. In days of a settled dynasty like our own, it is hard to realise the apprehensions inspired by Marlborough's ascendancy. But in 1710 Oliver Cromwell had been dead little more than fifty years. Men were nearer to the Protectorate than we are to the great Reform Bill. All the circumstances of the Protectorate were living facts in the memory of the nation. There was nothing incredible or unimaginable in the notion of a great soldier seizing the authority of the State. Marl-

borough had acquired immense wealth ; the Emperor
had wished to make him Governor of the Austrian
Netherlands ; he was a Prince of the Empire ; he had, in
an unwise moment, pressed the queen to make him Cap-
tain-General for life.   So extraordinary a career was
thoroughly calculated to exalt his imagination and inflame his ambition.   It was true that he would have no
successor in the male line, and this, among other things,
made the shrewder Tories doubtful about the existence
of the boundless designs that were freely imputed to him
by the bulk of their party.   Such dark suspicions as these,
however, were not needed to establish the advantage of
pulling down the man who was the chief tower of Whig
strength.

The Opposition were quite as keenly alive to the
party aspects of the Peace as were the government.
They assailed the Treaties, Walpole among the foremost,
with a vehemence that has never been surpassed.
We were breaking, they said, our most solemn engagements with the allies.   We were betraying the Dutch.
We were still leaving the crowns of France and Spain on
the heads of two princes of the House of Bourbon.   We
had covered ourselves with dishonour ; we had flung
away the fruits of twelve years of struggle and of victory ;
and we had wantonly, shamefully, and wickedly rejected
the opportunity of once for all delivering Protestant
England and Protestant Holland from the pretensions at
once of the Most Christian and of the Most Catholic king.

Nobody can dispute that the Whigs had that supreme
object of parliamentary desire, a strong debating case.
The English government, in concealing from their allies
the negotiations which they were secretly carrying on

with the common enemy, acted with a degree of fraud and duplicity that was worthy of ancient Greece or mediæval Italy. Even Frederick the Great never did anything so base as the statesmen who sent their general to Holland with express instructions actually to checkmate their own ally on the very field of battle. Bolingbroke's methods must be stamped by every impartial historian with indelible infamy. The betrayal and abandonment of the Catalans was truly criminal. But on the merits, and viewed in the light of subsequent events, the Peace must be pronounced to have been the true policy. It is ridiculous to attribute to Bolingbroke or his party the fruits of the Peace. The fruits were gathered at Utrecht, but they had been secured by twelve years of war. The sacrifices of England were in some degree repaid by the extension of her possessions. She retained from Spain the famous rock of Gibraltar, Port Mahon, and the Isle of Minorca. France surrendered Nova Scotia, Newfoundland, and Hudson's Bay. The fortifications of Dunkirk were to be dismantled. By a provision which to-day is regarded with horror, England was to be allowed to supply the Spanish possessions in America with negro slaves. More respectable clauses were those which extorted from the bigoted king the release of subjects who had been cast into prison for their religion, and a definite recognition of the Protestant line in Great Britain, as well as the expulsion of the Pretender from French territory. Against these substantial gains were undoubtedly to be set the risks of some counterbalancing mischiefs. But the mischiefs never came to pass, and the way was made ready for that long period of European tranquillity with which

the name of Walpole is for ever so honourably bound
up.

Harley was the first of the four statesmen who, within
the next hundred years, ascended from the Speaker's
chair to be heads of government.[1]   When the Tory
administration was formed, the Treasury was put in
commission, but not many months later Harley, as has
already been stated, was made Lord High Treasurer; he
left the House of Commons, became the Earl of Oxford
and Mortimer, and finally received the distinction of the
Garter.

The ministers had come in upon the flood tide of a
great reaction.   Experience has often shown the dangers
of these triumphant situations.   The new men speedily
found themselves in difficulties.   The queen's design had
been to break up the Whig junto, to break up government by party, and by ending the war to destroy the
towering ascendancy of Marlborough.   Harley, during
three years of back-stairs intrigue, had instilled into her
troubled mind designs of no wider scope than this.   The
views of the new Parliament were very different.   They
had no patience with schemes of moderation and comprehension.   "We are plagued here," Swift wrote to
Stella, "with an October Club; that is, a set of above
a hundred Parliament men of the country, who drink

---

[1] The other three were Sir Spencer Compton, who as Lord Wilmington succeeded Walpole in 1742; Addington, who stepped
directly from Speakership to Premiership, in succession to Pitt in
1801; and William Grenville, who was Speaker for a few months
in 1789, and became Prime Minister in the short-lived government
of All the Talents in 1806.   The Duke of Wellington, according to
Croker (ii. 164), proposed to Manners Sutton that he should make
a Tory government in 1831.

October beer at home, and meet every evening in a
tavern near the Parliament, to consult affairs and drive
things on to extremes against the Whigs, to call the old
Ministry to account, and get off five or six heads. . . .
The queen, sensible how much she was governed by the
late Ministry, runs a little into the other extreme, and
is jealous in that point, even of those who got her
out of the others' hands." (18th February 1711.)
Between the jealous murmurs of these men of the
October Club who wanted the heads of their enemies,
and the pertinacity of the queen, who would nót stir
beyond the point first marked out for her, Harley had
a hard game to play, and it soon appeared that he was
not the man to play it.

The savage and unholy genius of Swift had appeared
early on the scene. Exasperated at the failure of his
Whig friends to fulfil their promises of church preferment, he had been willingly caught by the attentions and
the flatteries of the Tory chiefs. " We were determined
to have you," said St. John. " You were the only one
we were afraid of." So they had him, his potent mind,
his virile and ingenious style, his irony, his penetration,
his truculence, his hate—all was henceforth at the service
of his new patrons. The history of polemical journalism
records nothing more effective for their purpose than the
sallies for attack and for defence made by Swift, along
with Prior, Parnell, and Defoe, against forces which
counted Steele and Addison. Never before nor since
were so many authors of classics which the world will
not willingly let die, engaged on ephemeral pieces which
the world willingly lets die on the next morning.
Addison rose or fell from the ranks of letters to be a

Secretary of State and a Cabinet minister, but his ascent was due to milder and happier gifts than those which led to the elevation of his friend. Never before nor since in England has a journalist, or a pamphleteer, achieved the position of personal ascendancy which was Swift's under the Tory administration of Queen Anne. He was a central figure at levees and drawing-rooms, and the hero of the ministers' ante-room. He was asked to Cabinet dinners, they called him Jonathan, he drove down to Windsor alone with Harley in his coach, he thought he was in all the secrets. In truth he was the dupe of his great friends. They told him as much as was necessary for his pamphlets and his articles, and they told him no more. He never knew, for instance, of Prior's clandestine mission to France, and to the very last he positively denied that there had been a whisper of intrigue with the Court of St. Germains.

Swift tells how he dined with Bolingbroke and Harcourt at Harley's table in the infancy of their power, and he could not forbear taking notice of the affection they bore to one another. The first excitement of a new-made Cabinet is said to be singularly intoxicating. But it does not last. Swift speedily had the mortification of seeing this kindness between his friends first degenerate into indifference and suspicion, and then corrupt into the greatest animosity and hatred. The truth is evident from Swift's own accounts of Harley, in spite of the writer's strong and lasting partiality for him, that the Lord Treasurer had none of the gifts of a leader. He was hesitating, evasive, timid, promising what he did not perform, and full of repellent airs of discretion and reserve. Unlike Walpole afterwards, he had none

of the stout and lively energy, none of the resolute
and imperious vigour, that was required to baffle the
spirit of intrigue and cabal in the royal closet and his
own Cabinet. His carelessness offended Mrs. Masham,
the queen's favourite. He allowed the queen to become alienated and sullen, without making an effort
to remove the causes. He took no pains to please his
colleagues. His temper, he once told Godolphin, was
to go along with the company and give no incon-
venience. " If they should say Harrow-on-the-Hill or
by Maidenhead were the nearest way to Windsor, I
should go with them, and never dispute it, if that
would give content, and that I might not be pressed
to swear it was so." This was true enough of his words,
but he forgot that though he would not dispute about
the road, in act he was always scheming to withdraw the
lynch-pin and to upset the coach, and his travelling companions knew it. The Whig Lord Chancellor Cowper
notes in his diary how one day he was drinking healths
with Harley in some Tokay which was good but thick, and
how he said to Harley that his white Lisbon wine
would have been better, as being very clear. The
company took it for a jest at " that humour of his,
which was never to deal clearly or openly, but always
with reserve if not dissimulation, or rather simulation,
and to love tricks where not necessary, but from an inward
satisfaction he took in applauding his own cunning.
If any man was ever born under a necessity of being
a knave, he was." Without going to such lengths as
this, under the ordeal of leadership his colleagues found
out that his moderation was a cloak for pusillanimity ;
that his industry had sunk into the respectable assiduity

of a clerk; that his self-possession was no better than stolidity in disguise; and that all his airs of calculation, wisdom, and politic reserve were only a blind to shifty dulness. He was made angry and jealous by Bolingbroke's intrepidity and dispatch, for nothing is so irritating to a man who has much ambition with little industry, as the sight of energy and application in a real or a fancied rival. He soon presented to the world that most miserable of all sights, a minister called to direct great affairs, with the pitiful equipment of a mediocre judgment and a sluggish will. On the other hand, when the day of disgrace and peril came, Oxford showed both composure and courage. When his fall had become certain, Swift, notwithstanding grievances of his own against Oxford, praised him for fortitude and magnanimity, and maintained that he was the ablest and faithfullest minister and truest lover of his country that the age had produced.

The events of the last few months of the reign of Queen Anne from the autumn of 1713 to the summer of the following year, are a striking dramatic illustration of the trite moralities that spring from the vanity of human things. People assume that when men are concerned in high affairs, their motives must lie deep and their designs reach far. Few who have ever been close to public business, its hurries, chances, obscurities, egotisms, will fall in with any such belief. These very transactions draw from Swift the observation, so obvious, so useful, so constantly forgotten, what a lesson of humiliation it is to mankind to behold the habits and passions of men, otherwise highly accomplished, triumphing over interest, friendship, honour, and their own personal safety as well

as that of their country. If St. John, for example, had
been as sagacious and as honest as Walpole, he would
never have left the House of Commons. His power and
popularity in that assembly were immense, and he explained it in a famous sentence, which is perhaps as true
of the House of Commons to-day as it was then. "Men
there," he said, "grow, like hounds, fond of the man
who shows them game, and by whose halloo they are
used to be encouraged." The common account of the
two ministers is that Oxford was a trifler and Bolingbroke a knave. Bolingbroke's own theory was that
Oxford had no deep ambition and no policy beyond petty
objects of domestic aggrandisement, and he listened with
incredulous disgust while Oxford grew maudlin over his
claret in recounting the imaginary glories of his ancestral
house. Yet Bolingbroke, too, must have been a trifler
to quit the true scene of authority for the sake of reviv-
ing the historic honours of his family. He chose to
desire the title of an earl, partly because an earldom in
his name and family had lately become extinct, but still
more because Oxford had been raised to that rank.
This weak sacrifice of the substance of power for the
shadow of decoration, brought him nothing but mischief.
Swift had been called over from Dublin in the summer
of 1713 to try to compose their dissensions. He was
almost the only common friend who was left to them.
Towards the end of the year he thought he had done
wonders when he had contrived to get them to go to
an audience at Windsor together in the same coach,
without other company, and with four hours in which
to come to a good understanding. Two days after he
learned from them both that nothing was done. Some-

time in May (1714) Swift was sitting with Oxford
and Bolingbroke in Lady Masham's apartment at St.
James's, and after some hours of talk called out to the
Lord Treasurer that, since he now despaired of a reconciliation between them, he should leave London. Before
going he wished to ask them, first, whether these mischiefs might not be remedied in two minutes; and next,
whether on the present footing the Ministry would not
be infallibly ruined in two months. Bolingbroke said
yes to both questions; but the Treasurer, "after his
manner, evaded both, and only desired me to dine with
him next day." Swift abruptly refused the dinner, and
at once departed into Berkshire. There he remained
until all was over. No domestic business was done, and
no attention was paid to affairs abroad. Each day
witnessed a new plot. The rivals seem neither to have
respected themselves nor one another. Oxford and
Bolingbroke continued to eat and drink and walk together as if no disagreement existed, and when they
parted they used such names of one another as only politicians could have borne without cutting one another's
throats. Even at the very end, the pair supped together
at Lady Masham's after one of their most violent quarrels. It is almost incredible that ministers with such
issues at stake, nursing serious purposes in their minds,
and with the certainty of the crisis being close at hand,
should have been capable of such lethargy and such
levity.

The truth is that the game, as Swift called it, was too
hard not only for Harley, but for all the rest of the dishonest band whom he had gathered around him. When
the hour of crisis at last arrived, even Bolingbroke, daring

and crafty as he seemed, was as much at sea as Harley
had ever been.   He wrote to Wyndham that nothing
was more certain than that there was at this time no
formed design in the party, whatever views some particular men might have, against the accession of King
George.   In the whole four years of his intimacy with
ministers, Swift vows that he never heard one single
word in favour of the Pretender.   The entire imputation
was nothing else but a device of opposition.   He often,
he says, asked men in the Whig camp whether they did
really suspect either the queen or her servants of having
favourable regards towards the Pretender, and they all
said no.   More particularly one person, afterwards in
great employment, frankly told him, "You set up the
Church and Sacheverell against us, and we set up Trade
and the Pretender against you."

Yet it is now beyond all doubt that both Oxford to a
certain extent, and Bolingbroke very deeply, were engaged in intrigues with the Pretender's agents.   Bolingbroke was quite aware of the desperate insecurity of a
restoration policy.   The public was in as inconsistent
a frame of mind as either Oxford or Bolingbroke.   As
Lord Stanhope has justly remarked, the country, with
wonderful blindness, resolutely adhered at the same
time to a Protestant king and to Jacobite ministers.
They prayed devoutly for the Electress Sophia, and
burnt in effigy the pope, the devil, and the Pretender;
yet they supported a Parliament that suffered no
step to be taken to the disadvantage of the most
dangerous member of the trinity.   On the other hand,
Bolingbroke saw that the Hanoverian accession meant
his own banishment from power, and the final over-

throw of his whole Church and Tory policy. The
Whigs had made themselves absolutely indispensable to
the House of Hanover, as Hanover was to them. The
only course, if Bolingbroke and his friends were to retain
power, or to return to it, lay in a reconciliation between
them and the Elector, and reconciliation was impossible.
Yet the statesman who had mastered all the inextricable
difficulties of Utrecht, might be excused for dreaming
that he was strong enough and adroit enough to overcome even the obstacles to a legitimist restoration.

In a sense it would be true to say that it was the
fidelity of the Tories to their Church that baulked the
legitimist plot, saved the Protestant succession, and
secured a parliamentary constitution. What men like
Swift, and the bulk of Tories more typical than
Swift, cared about was the Church. The Church was
to be preserved entire in all her rights, powers, and
privileges. All views on government condemned by
her were to be discouraged by law, and all schisms
and sects to be kept under due subjection. No
dissenter of any denomination was to be trusted with
the smallest degree of civil or military power; and no
Whig, low churchman, republican, moderation man, or
the like, was to receive any mark of favour from the
Crown. Why should not the Hanoverians be induced to
come into these views, and why should not ministers
make terms with them? Why should not the young
grandson of the Electress be invited over to be educated
in England, to learn our manners and language, and to
become acquainted with the true constitution in Church
and State?

Such counsel might well have tempted anybody ex-

cept the man who would have to execute it. Advice
of this kind, which would be perfectly wise if only some
vital condition happened to be totally different, is plen-
teously bestowed upon all party leaders in every generation. To make overtures to Hanover would be to give
deadly offence to the queen, and to exasperate the Tory
highfliers. It would be to run upon the rock that had
wrecked Oxford, and in effect to throw away the most
valuable weapon in the war against Oxford. Having no
settled principles either way, and moved solely by personal
ambition, Bolingbroke was driven towards Jacobitism by
the nature of the political position. Whether Bolingbroke
and Ormond were caballing with the agents of the Pretender merely with the view of procuring the dismissal
of Oxford and making sure of Jacobite support, or were
seriously aiming at a legitimist restoration, it was on
either theory the urgent duty of the Whigs to exercise
unsleeping vigilance. Happily for us they did not relax
nor falter, and happily for Walpole the peril and distraction of that time made so deep a mark on his party,
that almost to the close of his career he always found a
potent argument for party fidelity at a pinch, in a
reminder of the last four years of Queen Anne.

The Tories pressed on their policy. They had secured
the Peace and destroyed Marlborough. They had
strengthened the landed interest by the Act (1711)
which required every knight of the shire to have six
hundred pounds a year from land, and every burgess to
have three hundred from land. By a singularly disgraceful bargain between some Whigs and the Tory
malcontents of what would now be called the Extreme
Right, Parliament had at length passed the bill against

occasional nonconformity. The Presbyterian could no longer become the mayor of his town or the sheriff of his county by a formal compliance with an invidious test. This was not all. Bolingbroke, himself a Deist or less, in conjunction with Atterbury, who was a high churchman and more, now crowned the edifice of intolerance and exclusion by the Schism Act, practically prohibiting the dissenters from educating their own children. Walpole led a vehement resistance to this odious measure, but in vain. The dissenters were thus prevented from keeping public or private schools. They were shut out from the universities. By the law against occasional conformity, they were shut out from the corporations. If Bolingbroke could have had time to deprive them of the parliamentary franchise, and of the right of sitting in the House of Commons, he would have completed his grand object. The landed gentry and the Crown would have become the possessors of supreme authority, and the party system would have been extinguished by the permanent instalment of one party in power. The position was curiously like that of the Duke de Broglie and the party of moral order and Christian monarchy in 1873.

The end arrived with dramatic swiftness. The favourite declared against Oxford; she told him roundly that he never had done the queen any service, and that he never would. The queen was slow to act. The fatal irresolution, said Bolingbroke, which was inherent in the Stuart race hung about her. At length her torpid will was roused, and she broke into bitter reproaches against the minister. On one of the last days of July (1714) an angry scene took place between Bolingbroke and Oxford

in the very presence of the sovereign. The Lord
Treasurer was commanded to deliver up the white staff
of his office. He had been led to expect that his fall
would be broken by a dukedom and a pension; he got
neither, but was dismissed peremptorily and with every
circumstance of ignominy and mortification. But Bolingbroke's triumph was short. The queen, bewildered,
stunned, and worn out by the animosity and confusion
that raged around her, suffered an apoplectic seizure.
For five days she lay at Kensington only half-conscious.

The country was in keen suspense, with all the omens
of a rapidly approaching civil war. There was a revival
of the temper of 1682, when the Whigs, in disgust at
the actual oppressions of Charles II and the threatened
tyranny of James, had revolved plans of open rebellion,
and prepared risings in arms at London, Bristol, and
Newcastle. French refugee officers were ready to act
under the orders of General Stanhope. Marlborough,
then at Antwerp, was persuading the Dutch to send
ships and men to aid the Protestant cause. He had
made his preparations for an invasion, though it is doubtful whether he was not more likely to play the part of
General Monk than of William the deliverer. In the
Tory camp there was equal alertness. The military posts
were manned by officers of the right principles. Bolingbroke prepared his list of appointments. He was for
a government exclusively of Jacobites, including Bishop
Atterbury as Lord Privy Seal. The French minister
says that Bolingbroke assured him that all his measures
were so well taken, that within six weeks there would
have been no fear of the result. Yet at this very
moment he had a meeting at his house in Golden Square

with Walpole, Pulteney, and Stanhope. When the moment of crisis arrived, he was still drifting. A gentleman came up post haste from Cheshire. "Well, my lord," he said to Bolingbroke, "what is to be done?" The eager partisan found his leader in a palsy of indecision.

The queen had no further part to play on the sublunary stage. The white staff had not yet been settled. On Friday, 30th July, the political committee of the Privy Council, sitting at the Cockpit at Whitehall, were summoned to Kensington by urgent representations of the queen's dangerous condition. While they were seated, two Whig peers, the Dukes of Argyll and Somerset, entered the room. As Privy Councillors they were within their technical right, though the fact of their using it shows how little the modern practice of the Cabinet was yet established. The physicians were summoned, and they reported that the queen's case was desperate. It was then agreed to recommend her to appoint the Duke of Shrewsbury to be Lord Treasurer. There is some reason for supposing that this step was taken on the proposition of Bolingbroke himself. He had perceived some time before that his character was too bad to carry the great ensign of power, but he felt that his ability would secure supreme authority whether with or without the wand. They approached the bedside of the dying sovereign. Rousing herself from her lethargy, she handed to Shrewsbury the white staff for which, or for the power of which it was the emblem, so many great men have been willing to barter away their souls. According to current story she handed it to him with the one regal

utterance of her dismal life : she hoped that he would
hold it for the good of her people.   Another story is
that as she lay dying, she uttered several times the
hopeless cry of remorseful affection, "Oh, my brother,
my dear brother !"   She only lived a day longer.
"Sleep," wrote Arbuthnot to Swift, "was never more
welcome to a weary traveller than death to her."   To
Swift also Bolingbroke wrote, two days after the cup
had been dashed from his lips : "The Earl of Oxford
was removed on Tuesday ; the queen died on Sunday.
What a world is this, and how does fortune banter us."
"It is true, my lord," replied Swift ; "the events of five
days last week might furnish morals for another volume
of Seneca."   The artful fabric of policy and of party, in
which all the crafty calculations, the fierce passions, the
glowing hopes and confident ambitions of so many busy,
powerful, and ardent minds had been for four years
so eagerly concentrated, was in a single moment
dashed to pieces.   A century and a quarter elapsed
before a queen again reigned over the British realm.
The next memorable historic scene within the walls
of the palace at Kensington was on that summer
morning in 1837, when the young Princess Victoria,
before a captain as great as Marlborough, and counsellors
of a higher and purer stamp than the baffled intriguers
who hovered round the deathbed of Anne, went through
the first ceremonial of the most fortunate reign in
English history.

CHAPTER III

THE NEW REIGN—WHIG SCHISM

THE accession of the house of Hanover in the person of the great-grandson of James I. was once called by a Whig of this generation the greatest miracle in our history. It took place without domestic or foreign disturbance. Louis XIV was now in his seventy-eighth year, and his orb was sinking over a weak, impoverished, and depopulated kingdom. Even he did not dare to expose himself to the hazards of a new war with Great Britain. Within our own borders a short lull followed the sharp agitations of the last six months. The new king appointed an exclusively Whig Ministry. The office of Lord Treasurer was not revived, and the title disappears from political history. Lord Townshend was made principal Secretary of State, and assumed the part of first Minister. Mr. Walpole took the subaltern office of paymaster of the forces, holding along with it the paymastership of Chelsea Hospital. Although he had at first no seat in the inner Council or Cabinet, which seems to have consisted of eight members, only one of them a commoner, it is evident that from the outset his influence was hardly second to that of Townshend

himself. In little more than a year (October 1715) he
had made himself so prominent and valuable in the
House of Commons, that the opportunity of a vacancy
was taken to appoint him to be First Commissioner of
the Treasury and Chancellor of the Exchequer. Lord
Halifax and Lord Carlisle had in turn preceded him in
the latter office. Since Walpole, save for a few months
after Stanhope accepted a peerage in 1717, and before
Aislabie succeeded him in 1718, the Chancellor of the
Exchequer has always been in the House of Commons,
a change that marked one further stage in the growing
ascendancy of the representative and the taxing chamber.

Historians have sometimes urged that Townshend
and Walpole ought now to have advised the king to
bring a section of Tories into the Ministry. At that
date, at any rate, a policy of inclusion seems to have
been practically out of the question. Passion had risen
to far too high a degree of heat and violence to allow of
the composition of a mixed government, even if a mixed
government had been desirable. But in the interest of
the national settlement, nothing could have been less
desirable. A struggle for life and death had just been
brought to a good end, less by design or concert than
by the fortunate accident of the demise of the queen. It
would have been irrational to expect men who had
only a few weeks before been ready to resort to armed
force against one another, and who had just been risking
their estates and their heads on a great and decisive
issue, now at a moment's notice to sit down in amity
round the new king's council table. Even if the Whig
leaders had been free from personal repugnance, and the
Tory leaders had been willing to come into the combina-

tion, it would have been the height of infatuation to
prepare to face wavering Parliaments and a visibly
approaching insurrection, with a divided, lukewarm, or
uncertain Cabinet.   Experience both before and after
Walpole's era was entirely adverse to mixed governments.   William III tried it on two occasions, and each
time it was the judgment of the best observers that the
admission to place of men of doubtful allegiance only
added to his troubles.   Anne tried it from 1704 to
1708, and Marlborough and Godolphin found the failure
complete.   George II tried it when Walpole had disappeared, and no attempt to make a strong government
was less successful than that made on the principle of
the Broad Bottom.   If ever there was a time when
comprehension, even on a small scale, would have been
at once perilous and futile, it was the quarter of a
century after the accession of the House of Hanover.

Besides excluding their opponents from power, the
Whigs instantly took more positive measures.   The new
Parliament was strongly Whig.   A secret committee was
at once appointed to inquire into the negotiations for
the Peace.   Walpole was chairman, took the lead in its
proceedings, and drew the report.   The topics of the
report were such as at the present day would figure in
a motion of censure.   They are a recapitulation of all
the objections to be urged against the terms of the
Peace.   Every objection was supported by extracts from
authentic documents.   Walpole took five hours in reading
the report to the House, and the clerk at the table read
it over again on the following day.   It is a great political
indictment, charging the queen's ministers with deserting
their allies and betraying the honour and the interests of

the realm. The only truly criminal part of the accusation, that which related to secret transactions with the Pretender, breaks down, and was felt to have broken down. The intrigue was undoubted, but the intriguers and their confederates had been too discreet to leave dangerous papers behind in their desks. The evidence that would have condemned them was then hidden in the despatch-boxes at St. Germains.

Impeachment, however, was still naturally regarded as the proper process against ministers who had gravely offended a triumphant majority. It was the only way then known of securing responsibility to Parliament. A Tory House in 1701 impeached Somers, Halifax, Oxford, and Portland, for the part they had taken in the Spanish Partition Treaties of 1700. A Whig House now (1715) directed the impeachment of Oxford, Bolingbroke, and Ormond for high treason, and other high crimes and misdemeanours mainly relating to the Peace of Utrecht. When Walpole himself fell, a generation later (1742), there was a loud and sanguinary cry that he should be impeached. But even by that time this way of striking a political delinquent was beginning to seem anomalous. The proceedings against Oxford and Bolingbroke are the last instance in our history of a political impeachment. They are the last ministers who were ever made personally responsible for giving bad advice and pursuing a discredited policy, and since then a political mistake has ceased to be a crime. Warren Hastings was impeached (1788), and so was Lord Melville (1804), but neither case was political, for Hastings was charged with misgovernment, and Melville with malversation of official funds. Burke said in 1770 that impeachment was

dead, even to the very idea of it, and later history has
shown that he was substantially in the right. The
explanation of the disappearance of this old political
expedient is twofold. A refinement in men's sense
of equity gradually disclosed the hardship of punishing
ministers for acts that Parliament and the sovereign had
approved; and second, the remarkable growth of the
Cabinet system, of which I shall have something to say
on a later page, tended slowly but decisively to substitute the joint responsibility of the whole body of
ministers for the personal responsibility of an individual
minister. To impeach, or to pass an Act either of
attainder or of pains and penalties against, a whole
Cabinet would be practically absurd and impossible.

Walpole's share in pressing for these strong measures
against his fallen enemies is matter of some doubt.
Bolingbroke charges him with being their hottest advo-
cate. There is no positive evidence either way. Walpole was a man of humane and moderate temper, but he
was by no means a man averse to strike if he thought a
blow required. Though he had no rancour by nature,
he knew how to be relentless as a matter of business.
He had been the leader in sifting the evidence before
his secret committee. When somebody prophesied that
the committee would end in smoke, Walpole vehemently
cried out that he wanted words to express his sense of
the villany of the late Frenchified ministry. To us, to
whom impeachment is almost as much of an antiquity as
ordeal by fire, and in whom the Treaty of Utrecht
excites only historic interest and no passion, the whole
proceeding may seem intemperate and impolitic. Yet a
cool and sagacious bystander may very easily have

thought differently.   The country was in many parts
unsettled.   The proclamation of King George had been
in some places attended by riot and disorder.   The
Church was violent against the House of Hanover.
London was so uncertain that, for long after the accession, cannon were kept at Whitehall to keep the mob in
awe.   The Highlanders were rising.   It was in conformity to the political notions of the time, as it is to those
of our own time in relation to Ireland, to strike vindictive blows of this kind.   Such considerations as these
may well have had their weight in the ministerial decision.   The affair came to an abortive end.   After
Oxford had lain a year in the Tower, it was resolved
to reduce the charges against him from high treason to
misdemeanour ; and after another year a difference arose,
or was promoted by Walpole's connivance, between the
Lords and the Commons as to the mode of procedure.
After a prolonged exchange of explanations, the Commons resolved to drop the prosecution (1717).

The opening years of the new reign mark one of the
least attractive periods in political history.   George I.
was silent, simple, and not ill-meaning ; he was attentive
to business, thrifty, and pacific.   He had some ambition
to play a high and stately part, if he had only known
how.   But he cared very little for his new kingdom, and
knew very little about its people or its institutions.   He
brought over with him a couple of rapacious mistresses
and a swarm of courtiers, eager for the milk and honey of
the promised land.   It is not surprising that violent feuds
should have speedily arisen between this crew of greedy
strangers and the home-bred minister from Norfolk.
Walpole coarsely said of Schulenberg, afterwards Duchess

of Kendal, and the elder of the two royal favourites, that she was of so venal a nature that she would have sold the king's honour for a shilling advance to the highest bidder. The spirit of jobbery was insatiable. The office of master of the horse was left vacant, and the duchess received the salary. No master of the buck-hounds was appointed: the emolument went into a German pocket. When Walpole remonstrated with the king against these outrageous venalities, the king with a smile replied in the bad Latin in which, as neither of them knew the language of the other, he and his minister were said to converse together: "I suppose that you are also paid for your recommendations."

The manners of the outlandish invaders were as bad as their morals. One of them once carried his insolence so far that Walpole, though he was in the royal presence, summoning both the Latin and the frankness that he had learned at Eton, cried out to the offender, "*Mentiris impudentissime.*" His worst enemy was Robethon, the king's French secretary. "This man," said Walpole, "—a mean fellow, of what nation I know not—having obtained the grant of a reversion, which he designed for his son, I thought it too good for him, and therefore reserved it for my own son. On this disappointment the foreigner impertinently demanded 2500*l.*, under pretence that he had been offered that sum for the reversion, but I was wiser than to comply with his demands." Townshend was equally resolute in resisting the importunities of the two favourite ladies for English peerages, for reversions, grants, and all the rest of the perquisites which the Hanoverians regarded as their rightful spoil. The inevitable result was the growth of a bitter enmity in the minds of the king's favourite advisers and companions, and its gradual transfusion into the mind of the king himself.

Another source of danger to ministers sprang up within. Rival ambitions began to appear in the Whig camp almost as soon as the administration was formed. Townshend and Walpole stood together. They came from the same county, they had been at the same school, and Townshend had married Walpole's sister. Like Walpole, Townshend was a solid man, apt in business, assiduous, and firm, but unlike Walpole in being hot, impulsive, and impatient. The elevation of the two new ministers is said to have given umbrage to the ambition of Sunderland. His contemporaries could not agree whether the third Earl of Sunderland was quite so bad a man as his father, the faithless and unprincipled minister of James II. He hid violent passions under an austere and frigid demeanour; he sought no friends, and he affected to regard books as the only worthy companions of lofty natures. He formed an important collection of early and rare editions of the Greek and Latin classics at Althorp, destined in a later generation to become the home of still nobler and more splendid treasures. Sunderland fell short of money, and with a pang that none but a bibliomaniac can know, he transferred his beloved books for a sum of ten thousand pounds to his father-in-law, the Duke of Marlborough, in whose hands they became the foundation of the great Blenheim Library, dispersed not many years ago. Among other effects of Sunderland's classical reading, it had made him a fiery republican. He even thought fit to entertain Queen Anne with injurious reflections on the wickedness of princes.　Sunderland was clever, busy, and persevering, and he was thought to be the greatest intriguer since his father.　He was described besides as being "not only the most intriguing, but the most passionate man of his time."　Walpole was once asked why he never came to an understanding with Sunderland. "You little know Lord Sunderland," he replied.　"If I had so much as hinted at it, his temper was so violent that he would have done his best to throw me out of the window."　Something deeper, however, than temper divided the Sunderland Whigs from Walpole.　Aristocratic pride in union with republican professions has often produced the narrowest type of oligarch; and Sunderland's republicanism only meant that the wings of royal prerogative were to be clipped for the benefit of a small caste of exclusive patricians.　He hated the Crown, but he had none of Walpole's respect and inclination for the Commons.　It was no wonder that they soon fell out.

Walpole once remarked how difficult it is to trace the causes of a dispute between statesmen.　Some transactions of our own day furnish a striking illustration of the truth of this remark, and the difficulty of explaining such disputes would be most readily admitted by those who might seem to hold the clue.　Walpole's biographer maintains that it was Sunderland's discontent and Stanhope's weakness and bad faith that lay at the bottom of the Whig schism of 1717.　Stanhope's descendant, the careful historian of those times, insists that the rupture was due to Townshend's unreasonableness and want of judgment.　It is not possible at this distance of time, and with imperfect material, conclusively to

settle the question.   The king hated his son, and the
Prince of Wales was bent on making a party of his own
against his father.   The foreigners hated the English
ministers, and the ministers were stubbornly set against
the demands of the foreigners.   The Cabinet was divided
by no serious dissent on principle or policy, but by the
even more dangerous element of personal jealousy and
dissatisfied ambition.   All these conditions united to
make schism inevitable.

The king left his new dominion for Hanover in July
1716.   His passion for his native land, like his ignorance
of the tongue of the land that had adopted him, was a
piece of good fortune for constitutional government.
His inability to speak English led to that important
change in usage, the absence of the sovereign from
Cabinet Councils.   His expeditions to Hanover threw
the management of all domestic affairs almost without
control into the hands of his English ministers.   If the
two first Hanoverian kings had been Englishmen instead
of Germans, if they had been men of talent and ambition,
or even men of strong and commanding will without
much talent, Walpole would never have been able to
lay the foundations of government by the House of
Commons and by Cabinet so firmly that even the ob-
durate will of George III was unable to overthrow it.
Happily for the system now established, circumstances
compelled the first two sovereigns of the Hanoverian
line to strike a bargain with the English Whigs, and it
was faithfully kept until the accession of the third George.
The king was to manage the affairs of Hanover, and the
Whigs were to govern England.   It was an excellent
bargain for England.

Smooth as this operation may seem in historic description, Walpole found its early stages rough and
thorny. The first royal visit to the electoral dominions
speedily brought to light the perils that lay alike in the
hatred between father and son, and in the rivalry among
ministers. The double leaven soon began to work. The
Hanoverians played upon the king's jealousy of the
prince, and rapidly instilled into his mind the suspicion
that Townshend and his colleagues were intriguing with
Argyll and the prince's party in England. It is as
certain as anything can be in matters so obscure and
intricate, that for this charge there was no foundation,
and that Walpole was justified in assuring Stanhope,
with wholesome bluntness, that whoever sent over the
accounts of any intrigues of this kind, or any management in the least tending to any view or purpose but
the service, honour, and interest of the king, would be
discovered to be " confounded liars from the beginning
to the end."

Nor was it possible to cut off the politics of Hanover
from the politics of Great Britain. The acquisition of
Bremen and Verden from Sweden for the electorate of
Hanover, was approved by Walpole on the ground that
the two provinces commanded the only inlets from
British waters into Germany. They secured the trade
with Hamburgh, and put a check on the molestation by
Sweden of British commerce in the Baltic. When the
king, however, for Hanoverian reasons sought to make
war on the Czar of Russia, because he had invaded the
Grand Duchy of Mecklenburg, Townshend declared that
the nation would never consent to make sacrifices for
interests that were none of theirs, and Walpole vowed

that he could not raise the money. The king was furious, and his exasperation at being thwarted in his warlike designs was artfully inflamed by hints that the ministers in England were secretly striving to exalt the Prince of Wales, and to show that the business of Parliament could be as well transacted by the son as by the father.

A pretext was found for the removal of Townshend from his office, in circumstances which it is not worth while here to recapitulate. They would never have been deemed adequate cause for so strong a step, if other motives had not operated, and it is impossible to acquit either Sunderland or Stanhope of singular disloyalty to their friends and colleagues in London. Walpole had described the situation in a private letter to Stanhope at Hanover : "The prince hates us, and at the same time we are almost lost with the king, having all the foreigners determined against us." Even the loosest form in which we can imagine the great and honourable conception of loyalty among members of a Cabinet, as it is now held, would condemn the action of the two ministers at Hanover in lending themselves to the king's designs against absent colleagues. In the sharp recriminations that were exchanged between Stanhope and Walpole, the former takes up ground with which it is impossible to feel satisfied. Was he, Stanhope asks, to tell the king that Townshend must continue to be Secretary of State, or else that the Whigs would quit office in a body ? "I really have not yet learnt to speak such language to my master ; and I think a king is very unhappy if he is the only man in the nation who cannot challenge any friendship from those of his subjects

whom he thinks fit to employ." It will be observed
that the question raised by Stanhope touches an
essential part of Cabinet government. Is the king to
exercise unfettered choice in the distribution or redistribution of offices? Even if we assume that they are
taken exclusively from one party, is he to command
the services of individual leaders at his own discretion,
and to assign them their respective offices as to him
may seem good? Queen Anne had undoubtedly acted
on this principle. Walpole thought that the time had
come for ministers to settle their offices among
themselves.

Townshend was prevailed upon for a very short time
to remain in the administration as Lord Lieutenant of
Ireland, then always a Cabinet office. But the truce
did not last. The king's favour had too evidently gone
to Sunderland and Stanhope. On the proposal that the
Commons should vote supplies for preparations against
Sweden, the Townshend Whigs showed themselves cold
and disaffected; Walpole spoke coldly for the vote, but
lent it no active support; and it was only carried by a
majority of four. In his resentment at this narrow
escape of a government measure, the king dismissed
Townshend from his post the same night. Walpole was
too valuable at the Treasury to be so lightly parted
with. Vain attempts were made to separate him from
his colleague. The tender of his resignation the next
morning was followed by an extraordinary scene in the
royal closet. The king entreated him not to retire, and
put the seals back into his hat. Walpole protested that
if as Chancellor of the Exchequer he found money for
the warlike designs of Stanhope and Sunderland, he

would lose his credit and reputation; and if, on the
other hand, he resisted them, then he would forfeit the
gracious favour of his sovereign. No fewer than ten
times were the seals replaced upon the table. The king
at length gave way, and Walpole quitted the closet with
tears in his eyes, leaving his master as painfully agitated
as himself.

There was one quarter in which the split in the
Whig party and the fierce quarrel in the royal family
stirred the liveliest delight. Atterbury, the conspirator
who then held the episcopal see of Rochester, was now,
under elaborate disguise of cypher and cant names,
writing to the Pretender sanguine accounts of what
was going on at court. From these letters we learn
how high the Jacobite hopes were raised by the removal
of the two ministers who were well known to be the fastest
friends of the present settlement. Every piece of gossip
about the dissensions between the Prince of Wales and
the Duke of Hanover, as they styled King George, was
magnified into a reason for the fond belief, which only
the inveterate fatuity of plotters in exile could have
entertained, that the king would rather throw the
British crown to the Pretender than suffer it to devolve
on his detested heir. Every movement of the public
funds sent their spirits up or down, as if they were
bears on a stock exchange. The Tories were as elated
as the pure Jacobites. They flattered themselves that
the Whigs were so divided, that nothing short of another
rebellion could bring them together again. The city
Whigs, ignorant of the personal intrigues behind the
scenes, and bewildered by such rapid changes in administration, were all anxiety to know what they could mean.

The truth is that the Whigs were in so great a majority that, like all parties in such circumstances, they could afford moderate quarrels among themselves. The famous Septennial Act of 1716 had secured their parliamentary majority for some years to come. It had once been among the prerogatives of the Crown to retain the same Parliament during the life of the sovereign, and Charles II did actually keep his last Parliament for seventeen years. Such excess produced reaction, and in 1694 Parliament passed an Act limiting its normal lifetime to periods of three years. In 1716 the great exigencies of the time justified a move in the other direction, and an extension of the life of a Parliament from three years to seven. The measure, which was originally designed for the special object of securing the Protestant succession at a moment of peril, had wider consequences. Speaker Onslow, the sage observer of parliamentary events, used to declare that the Septennial Bill of 1716 marked the true era of the emancipation of the House of Commons from its former dependence on the Crown and the House of Lords.[1] The Act was undoubtedly one of the most important causes of the increase of that power in the House of Commons, on which Walpole was the first minister habitually and on principle to rely. Meanwhile it enabled the Whigs in 1717 to cut themselves in two with impunity.

After leaving court in 1717, Walpole remained in opposition for three years. Many blamed him for deserting the king. Many declared that it was desertion of the country and of Parliament to abandon schemes for reducing the national debt, which, as he

[1] Coxe, i. 137.

was well aware, no successor had the ability to carry
through. Walpole protested, as so many men since
have protested in the same circumstances, that nothing
was further from his mind than to embarrass government.
But when men leave colleagues in a government, they
seldom see how far their departure may lead them. The
spirit of party, and the restlessness of a powerful nature,
were too strong for the practice of benevolent neutrality.
While loudly disclaiming any desire to embarrass the
king's ministers, he still found himself invariably compelled bitterly to resist all their measures. He opposed
the Mutiny Bill, though its provisions were merely
formal and were necessary. He opposed the repeal of
the Schism Act, though he had himself once denounced
it as more worthy of Julian the Apostate than of the
Protestant Parliament of England. So apt is party
spirit to degenerate into moral paradox.

Yet none of these excesses or inconsistencies shook
his hold on Parliament. Nor is that hold hard to
understand. To begin with, he showed upon occasion
the moderating temper which the House of Commons
always secretly respects, even in its moments of passion
and of heat, and which it always recognises when the
heat has evaporated. A member had greatly offended
the House, by bringing against a certain set of men that
charge of obstruction which has become part of the
common form of party scolding in later days. A few
words from Walpole were enough to save the gentleman
from being sent to the Tower. Shippen, the Jacobite
leader, said of the king's speech that it seemed rather
calculated for the meridian of Germany than of Great
Britain, and regretted his Majesty's ignorance of our

language and our constitution. The House was furious at this uncourtly plainness, but Walpole composed the angry waves, and "honest Shippen" would easily have escaped, if his honesty had not taken the form, as honesty sometimes does, of obstinate contumacy. But the true basis of Walpole's power was something more positive than a moderating temper. He was a skilful manager of men, but he was also an unrivalled man of business. Wherever money was concerned, his knowledge, skill, clearness, and judgment gave him an authority that was paramount. In all these transactions, even his worst enemies had with mortification to admit that the House of Commons relied more upon Walpole's opinion than upon that of any other member. In weighing the ordinary accusation that his immense parliamentary influence was due to gross corruption, it is well not to forget that he laid the foundations of that influence while he was in opposition and without strong party support, and without any of the means of corruption. The truth is that the House of Commons has always been most wisely ready to give its confidence to men whom it believes to possess a firm, broad, and independent grasp of the great material interests of the country.

The time was close at hand when neglect of Walpole's practical wisdom brought upon the nation a terrible disaster. Before this catastrophe arrived, Walpole was provoked to the exertion of all his powers by a proposal of the gravest constitutional moment. Sunderland was in extreme disfavour with the Prince of Wales, and he was well aware that the death of the reigning king would at once lead to his own dismissal. The centre of gravity was still in the Upper House, where the Whigs had a standing majority : the prince's first step, therefore, on coming to the throne would be to strengthen the Tory minority in the House of Lords. Queen Anne had set him a precedent in the creation of the twelve peers to carry the Peace of Utrecht. That this was a violent act, honest Tories admitted, but they declared that, after all, it was not to be compared with the act by which the Commons, chosen by the people for three years, chose themselves for seven. Sunderland did not shrink from taking an audacious measure to counterwork the danger in advance. Lord Stanhope was made to bring in a bill for putting a close restriction on the royal prerogative of making . peers. The number of peers, according to the bill, was never at any time to be enlarged beyond six over the number then existing. At the accession of George I. the total number of the peers, including the twenty-six peers spiritual and the sixteen representative peers from Scotland, was two hundred and seven.[1] Instead of the sixteen elective members from Scotland, twenty - five from that kingdom were to be made hereditary. Where a failure of issue male occurred, it might be filled up by new creation in England, and by selection from other members of the peerage in Scotland. Obviously, if such a measure had become law, it would have transformed the House of Lords into a close college, and the peerage would have become an unchangeable caste. The Lords would have acquired a fixed prepon-

[1] At the accession of William IV the number, including the addition of thirty-two temporal and spiritual peers from Ireland, had risen to three hundred and ninety. (Stanhope's *History of England,* c. ii. 44.) To-day the members of the House of Lords are five hundred and sixty.

derance of power over Crown and Commons alike;
for while the Crown could coerce the Commons by a
dissolution, and the Commons could restrain the Crown
by refusal of supplies, the Lords would have been
beyond the reach of either of the other two branches of
the legislature.

That this far-reaching measure failed to become law,
is due to Walpole's penetration and rapidity, and by
hardly any other action of his life did he set a deeper
stamp upon our system of government. Formidable
difficulties were in his way. The king might have been
expected to object to a limitation of one of the most
cherished of royal prerogatives. But the king hated
the Prince of Wales, and was as anxious as Sunderland
to clip his wings. The Scotch peers were won by the
prospect of exchanging an elective for a hereditary seat.
The Lords as a whole were openly or privately gratified
by a measure which, in limiting their numbers, augmented
their individual importance. The bill engaged the
talents of the two most delightful prose writers of the
day. It was defended by Addison, in what proved to
be the final task of his life, and it was attacked by Steele.
Why could not faction, says Johnson, find other
advocates? Controvertists cannot long retain their
kindness for each other, and "every reader must surely
regret that these two illustrious friends, after so many
years passed in confidence and endearment, in unity of
interest, conformity of opinion, and fellowship of study,
should finally part in acrimonious opposition." The
spirit of faction was too busy and too hot for these
pensive regrets, and no effort was spared to forward the
ministerial design. The king's name was freely used.

Sunderland told everybody that the king wished the bill ;
that the Prince of Wales would otherwise do mad things
when he came to the throne ; that if the Whigs rejected
it, their party would be for ever undone. Bribes and
threats were employed with equal profusion. All this
took the heart out of the opposition Whigs. They held
a meeting at Devonshire House, where Walpole found
them lukewarm, indifferent, and out of spirits. He at
once took a high tone, protested against any weakness,
and used all the topics that are the common property in
all ages of all militant leaders of Opposition pressing
sluggish adherents to make a fight. Public opinion, he
said, was rising against the bill. The country gentlemen were waking up to the insult implied upon their
class by a measure which would shut the door of the
House of Lords in their faces. He had himself over-
heard a country gentleman with not more than eight
hundred pounds a year, vow with great warmth to
another country gentleman, that though he had no
chance of being made a peer himself, he would never
consent to lay his family under the ban of perpetual
exclusion. Finally, he used the universal and irresistible
clencher that it was a splendid opportunity of weakening
and discrediting the government. "Even if I am
deserted by my party," he said, winding up his animated
remonstrance, "I myself will singly stand forth and
oppose it." A lively altercation followed, but such
high and inspiriting firmness in a political leader with
an accepted character for judgment, is always sure to
carry the day. The party came over to Walpole's
opinion, and he further justified it by a speech whose
qualities the historian does not overrate in declaring it

to be one of the most eloquent and masterly ever delivered in the House of Commons, whether we judge it by the impressions of the time, or by the effect of the report of it upon our own minds.[1]

There is nothing in it comparable to that superb passage in which the greatest writer of the century in its last decade defended a natural aristocracy.[2] Nevertheless it is an excellent setting for what a first-rate judge of our own day used to describe as the very best parliamentary argument he knew, excepting Mr. Gladstone's speech on the taxation of charities. Walpole's reasoning, and the energy with which it was urged, led to the rejection of the bill by a triumphant majority of two hundred and sixty-nine against one hundred and seventy-seven.

[1] This famous speech is given in outline by Coxe, chap. xviii.
[2] *Appeal from the New to the Old Whigs*, p. 217 (ed. 1818).

CHAPTER IV

RISE TO POWER—BOLINGBROKE

To the great dismay of the Jacobites, the two circumstances on which they had been so fondly counting suddenly took a new turn. The Whig schism came to an end, and the king allowed himself to be reconciled to his son. Walpole played an active part in both of these transactions. As clearly as the Jacobites, he perceived that the feud between the prince and the king threatened real dangers to the peace of the realm. Things had reached such a pitch that the king actually consulted the Lord Chancellor as to the legality of a bill for compelling the Prince of Wales, on the demise of the crown, to divest himself of his German dominions. A much more sinister project was found among the king's papers at his death, nothing less than a proposal made by the head of the Admiralty to seize the Prince of Wales and carry him off to the wilds of America. This atrocious design recalls the old rumour that Buckingham had offered to oblige Charles II by kidnapping his consort, dispatching her to some colony, and then grounding a divorce on the plea of wilful desertion. Notwithstanding his hatred of his son, and his grim usage of his unfortunate wife, George I. was not the man to listen to a scheme of this kind. When Walpole at last prevailed upon the prince to send his father a submissive message, it was graciously received; the letter was followed by a visit to the king at St. James's, and to show that he and the sovereign were once more on terms, the prince was sent back to his house in Leicester Fields with a complimentary escort of life guards.

Walpole's return to the administration was part of the same political scheme, just as his fall twenty years later was connected with the position of the heir apparent of that day. A man of his energy and passion for the work of government is apt to grow tired of opposition, and public considerations pointed in the same way as his own ruling impulse. The end of the Whig schism involved a general closing up of ranks in face of new alarms from the Pretender. The reunion of the Whigs was at least as welcome to the men in office as to the men in opposition. The hand that had just destroyed the Peerage Bill was too heavy to be left with safety outside the government. Yet though Walpole and Townshend once more joined the administration, they were forced to content themselves with subordinate posts. Townshend, who had filled what was then the leading office of Secretary of State, became Lord President of the Council; and Walpole, who had been First Lord of the Treasury and Chancellor of the Exchequer, was made Paymaster of the Forces without a seat in the Cabinet (1720). His opposition was at an end, but he took no part in the active work of government, and in the summer withdrew to Norfolk to bide his time.

Before many months had passed the country was overtaken by the memorable disasters of the South Sea

Bubble. This famous project, which was indirectly the means of Walpole's ascendancy, had its origin in the same delusions about the fabulous wealth of Spanish America, that twenty years later led to the Spanish War and to Walpole's fall. France had been thrown into a frenzy of speculation by the Mississippi schemes of Law. The fever quickly spread to England, with a difference that may be worth noting, that while Law was a man of genius and by no means without sincerity and even elevation of character, in London the promoters were little more than ordinary stock-jobbers with extraordinary rashness, audacity, and corruption. The South Sea Act of 1720 was a measure for enabling the South Sea Company to absorb in their stock a quantity of irredeemable annuities, consolidate various branches of the public debt, reduce the rate of interest, and out of the profits of their trade eventually achieve one of the most eagerly desired objects of that day by paying off the national debt. Fortunately for himself Walpole had at a very early stage exposed the fallacies on which the plan of the directors rested, though he remained an inactive colleague of ministers who were its zealous supporters. Thousands of bubble projects have been launched since that memorable mania, and only a generation ago speculation in railway stock was almost as extravagant, widespread, and desperate as the great fever of 1721. But the South Sea scheme is in our history the only case of this ruinous calamity, at which a government directly and actively connived. When the crash came, a cry broke out for vengeance, as fierce and as indiscriminate as outcries usually are, when people are bent on punishing others for their own blindness and folly. One peer in his place demanded that, in the absence of any adequate penalty by existing law, the South Sea directors should be treated like parricides in ancient Rome, stitched up in sacks, and flung into the river; and on this occasion the peer was representative of the general judgment. Apart from the social confusion, the political danger was by no means slight. The German mistresses were known to have had a share in the spoil, the Prince of Wales had been chairman of a bubble copper company from which he extracted forty thousand pounds in a metal more precious than copper; and besides these specific grounds for anger, the natural tendency to blame government was especially strong when that government was new, foreign, unsettled, and unpopular.

All eyes were turned to Walpole. Though he had privately dabbled in South Sea stock on his own account, his public predictions came back to men's minds; they remembered that he had been called the best man for figures in the House, and the disgrace of his most important colleagues only made his sagacity the more prominent. Craggs, the Secretary of State, and his father, the Postmaster-General, were both implicated in the receipt of enormous sums, as the differences on transactions in fictitious stock created to buy the passing of the South Sea Bill. The son died of smallpox, and the father quickly followed, leaving a fortune of a million and a half. Aislabie, the Chancellor of the Exchequer, was down for nearly eight hundred thousand pounds, fraudulently acquired. Sunderland was charged with similar transactions, but whatever substance there may have been in the charge, they had been managed discreetly enough to leave a colourable excuse for acquitting him. Still public opinion made it impossible for Sunderland to retain office. Lord Stanhope, his principal colleague, was removed by a curiously sudden death in February 1721. In the course of an angry debate, the young Duke of Wharton compared Stanhope to Sejanus, the wicked minister who fomented divisions in the imperial family, and made the reign of Tiberius, his master, odious to the Roman people. Stanhope was so incensed at gibes that Walpole would only have laughed at, that in the angry transport of his reply he was seized with a fit, and the next day he expired. This brought about a re-casting of the ministerial parts, and at the request of the great territorial Whigs, Walpole undertook the task. He returned to his old posts, and once more became First Lord of the Treasury and Chancellor of the Exchequer (April 1721), while Townshend was again Secretary of State.

Walpole held his offices practically without a break for twenty-one years. The younger Pitt had an almost equal span of unbroken supremacy, but with that exception there is no parallel to Walpole's long tenure of power. To estimate aright the vast significance of this extraordinary stability, we must remember that the country had just passed through eighty years of revolution. A man of eighty in 1721 could recall the execution of Charles I., the protectorate of Oliver, the fall of Richard Cromwell, the restoration of Charles II, the exile of James II, the change of the order of succession to William of Orange, the reactionary ministry of Anne, and finally the second change to the House of Hanover. The interposition, after so long a series of violent perturbations as this, of twenty years of settled system and continuous order under one man, makes Walpole's government of capital and decisive importance in our history, and constitutes not an artificial division like the reign of a king, but a true and definite period, with a beginning, an end, a significance, and a unity of its own.

Parliamentary government has been said to prevent great shocks, but to multiply small ones. From the critical state of the time Walpole was ceaselessly exposed to these small shocks, and the vigour with which he circumvented the cabals that from the first year to the last surrounded and confronted him, was only less important to the security of the great public bulwark of his power, than the success with which he surmounted grave difficulties of state. It would have been easy for Walpole in South Sea affairs to avenge old grievances on Sunderland and others. As it was he chose the magnanimous course of insisting, even at the expense of much unpopularity for himself, on the most lenient counsels that Parliament could be persuaded to allow. But the jealous and unquiet Sunderland, even in the hour of his disgrace, was again busy on devices for displacing the new rival in the royal favour. He hit upon the extraordinary expedient of suggesting to the king that he should create Walpole Postmaster-General for life. His calculation was that the large pay would tempt a man of narrow fortune; that if Walpole accepted, he would be incapable of sitting in Parliament; while, if he refused, he would offend the king. The king, however, baulked the childish plan by asking whether Walpole desired the proposal or knew of it. Sunderland confessed that he did not. "Then," said the king, "do not make him the offer. I parted with him once against my inclination, and I will never part with him again, so long as he is willing to serve me."

The king may well have felt the perilous situation from which Walpole's capacity had rescued him. The discovery of the plot for which Atterbury was exiled (1722), revealed how high Jacobite hopes had risen during the recent confusion. In the excitement some measures were taken with Walpole's approval, which it is hard to justify. The bill of pains and penalties against Atterbury himself was a dangerous invasion of the security and sanctity of legal guarantees, and it is satisfactory to think that it is the last instance of its kind. Walpole appeared as a witness in the course of the proceedings; the bishop used all his skill to perplex his opponent; but, says Speaker Onslow, he was too hard for the bishop at every turn, "although a greater trial of skill this way scarce ever happened between two such combatants."[1] Still more alien, not only to the temper of to-day, but even to the better mind of that age, as Onslow's censures prove, was the imposition of a tax of 100,000*l.* on Roman Catholics as a composition for recusancy, and it was presently extended even to non-jurors. "The whole nation almost, men, women, and children capable of taking an oath, flocked to the places where the quarter sessions were holden. . . . It was a strange as well as a ridiculous sight to see people crowding to give a testimony of their allegiance to a government, and cursing them at the same time for giving them the trouble of so doing and for the fright they were put into by it; and I am satisfied more real disaffection to

[1] Coxe, *Original Papers*, i. 328.

the king and his family arose from it than from anything
which happened at that time."—(*Onslow*). The lesson
was not lost upon the minister ; for no administration of
the century, least of all that which closed the century,
exhibited less of the spirit of oppression and intolerance.

Sunderland died in 1722, and left as his representative in the public counsels a statesman whose name has
long ago faded away from general recollection, and who
made no great mark on national policy, but yet was by
the common consent of contemporaries unsurpassed by
any man of his age in brilliance of gifts, compass of
view, and aspiring vigour of character. Carteret was
by far the ablest and most striking representative of the
principles, policy, and temper in handling public business,
that were most directly antagonistic to the principles,
policy, and temper of Walpole. "He was a fine person,"
says Shelburne, who married his daughter, "of commanding beauty, the best Greek scholar of the age, overflowing
with wit, not so much a *diseur de bons mots*, as a man of
true, comprehensive ready wit, which at once saw to the
bottom, and whose imagination never failed him, and
was joined to great natural elegance. He had a species
of oratory more calculated for the senate than the people."[1]
It was Carteret who said to Henry Fox, "I want to
instil a noble ambition into you ; to make you knock
the heads of the kings of Europe together, and jumble
something out of it that may be of service to this
country." "What is it to me," he once said, "who is a

[1] *Shelburne's Life*, i. 38. Mr. Disraeli, who had brooded much
over Bolingbroke's period and his ideas, has some interesting remarks
on Carteret and Shelburne in *Sybil*, ch. 3. Oddly enough, while
talking of Carteret, the novelist says that Bolingbroke was the only
peer of his period who was educated. What of Chesterfield, too ?

judge or who is a bishop? It is my business to make
kings and emperors, and to maintain the balance of
Europe." He was all for glory, says Onslow, and thought
much more of raising a great name to himself all over
Europe, and having that continued by historians to all
posterity, than of any present domestic popularity or
renown whatever. A story is told of Carteret which
every lover of scholarship as a fine adornment of great-
ness in character or action, will always delight to remember. As he lay dying (1762) the Under-Secretary
took to him, as Lord President, the preliminary articles
of the Treaty of Paris. He found the minister so
languid, that he proposed to put off the business until
another day. Carteret replied by repeating the beautiful lines, where Sarpedon says to Glaucus that if keeping
back from the fray would keep back age and death from
them, then indeed neither would he himself fight amid
the foremost, nor send the other into the battle; "but
now—since ten thousand shapes of death hover over
us, and them no mortal may escape—now, forward
let us go." [1] The particular emphasis with which,
according to the narrator, he spoke forth the third line
—οὔτε κεν αὐτὸς ἐνὶ πρώτοισι μαχοίμην—was true
to a ruling passion which made him the most dangerous
of ministers, though no inglorious man.

Carteret was made Secretary of State by the influence

---

[1] ὦ πέπον, εἰ μὲν γὰρ πόλεμον περὶ τόνδε φυγόντες,
αἰεὶ δὴ μέλλοιμεν ἀγήρω τ' ἀθανάτω τε,
ἔσσεσθ', οὔτε κεν αὐτὸς ἐνὶ πρώτοισι μαχοίμην,
οὔτε κε σὲ στέλλοιμι μάχην ἐς κυδιάνειραν.
νῦν δ' (ἔμπης γὰρ κῆρες ἐφεστᾶσιν θανάτοιο
μυρίαι, ἃς οὐκ ἔστι φυγεῖν βροτὸν οὐδ' ὑπαλύξαι),
ἴομεν.   (*Iliad*, xii. 322-328.)

of Sunderland, and he took over from his first patron
his dislike to the two brother ministers.   A strenuous
conflict began between the two sections of the government, which ended in 1724 in Carteret's defeat.   This
has been commonly cited as an instance of Walpole's
jealous determination to exclude every superior man
from power—a charge on which it is sufficient to remark that Carteret was quite as busy in striving to
exclude Walpole and Townshend, as they were in excluding him; that Townshend had a much more active feeling,
and took a more active part than Walpole; that it was
an ordinary case of struggle in a Cabinet, in which,
luckily for the country, Carteret happened to have the
fortune of war against him; and, finally, that Walpole
would have stultified himself and ruined his whole policy
if he had allowed a minister to remain in charge of so
momentous a branch of business as foreign affairs, of
whom it could be truly said, as Onslow said of Carteret,
that "he thought consulting the interior interests and
disposition of the people, the conduct of business in
Parliaments, and the methods of raising money for the
execution even of his own designs, was a work below
his applications, and to be left as underparts of government to the care of inferior and subordinate understand-
ings, in subserviency, however, to his will and measures."
We need not impute to Walpole an insatiable thirst for
power, in order to understand his willingness to part company with a colleague of such temper as this.   It is to be
observed, further, that Walpole did not hurry to part
company with him, for Carteret remained a member of
the Cabinet for six years (1724-1730) after he ceased to
be Secretary of State.   To be able to work with a man

in a Cabinet for ten years, hardly indicates an arrogant aversion to all colleagues of genius.

It was important at this moment to send a strong man to Dublin, for Ireland was shaken by the dangerous agitation which had its origin in Wood's halfpence, but which had its roots much deeper than the mere issue of a patent to an English tradesman to supply a deficiency in Irish coinage. That the issue of the patent was an odious job, by which a large sum of money was to find its way into the pocket of the king's mistress, is undeniable. The amount to be struck was in gross and mischievous excess over what was required, as was shown by the willingness of the government to reduce the sum from more than one hundred thousand pounds to forty thousand. The whole operation was conducted from first to last with a flagrant disregard for Irish opinion or Irish authority, which might be called incredible, if the same principle had not prevailed until now. On the other hand, the unfortunate coins were good and of true value, nor was anybody obliged to take them who did not choose; and the case against them was marked by many exaggerations, misrepresentations, and lies.

Unluckily for the peace of the British government, the case was taken up by the strongest controversial genius of the age. Swift hated and despised the country in which his unhappy lot was cast, but he had the honest contempt natural to a powerful mind for the wretched system on which it was governed, and he was inspired besides by keen animosity against the party in England and the minister, by whose neglect or ill-will he had been doomed to perpetual exile. *The Drapier's Letters* are among the very few pieces of political controversy on an ephemeral incident, to which their literary qualities give lasting interest. The fourth of them reveals the real spring of the agitation—the old and ever-renewed protest against the government of Ireland by England. This was one of the too few occasions in Irish history on which the whole nation in both its branches, and of both creeds, spoke with one voice and faced their bad rulers with a united front. It was no feeling of justice, and no interest in good government in Ireland, that prompted the final surrender, but the fear, inspired in the agents of Ascendancy, that the exasperation against Wood and his coins was bringing Catholics and Protestants, Jacobites and Whigs, into an intimacy that was dangerous to the constitutional connection between Great Britain and the sister-kingdom. Walpole at once saw the impossibility of forcing the inclinations of a whole people, governed and governors alike. Carteret on the spot—though his own intrigues in Ireland at an earlier stage of the affair will hardly bear examination— now earnestly supported the same view, and, in spite of Townshend and others of their colleagues, the viceroy was authorised to announce to the Irish Parliament that the obnoxious patent was absolutely at an end. Ireland gave Walpole no further trouble. Affairs were mainly guided by the influence of Archbishop Boulter in the English and planter interest; and Walpole appears, when he thought of Ireland at all, to have regarded this as the safest policy.

With the temporary suppression of the Jacobite plots, the subjection of Carteret, the pacification of the ferment in Ireland, the minister found the course of domestic affairs run smoothly enough. Now and at all times it was foreign affairs that demanded most attention; but his policy in this department will be most conveniently viewed in a chapter of its own. The king wished to reward his minister by a peerage. Walpole was the first minister who made the House of Commons the centre of authority, and he declined to leave it. The peerage was conferred upon his eldest son. Among minor expedients for strengthening his influence was one at which philosophers may smile, and which the party leader may in his heart despise, but which for practical purposes he is not likely to overlook. In 1725 Walpole induced the king to revive the order of the Bath. No creation had been made since 1661. The minister bethought himself of it as a cheap way of rewarding a friend or buying off a possible foe. The bestowal of the red riband, moreover, would be convenient for staving off what is in every generation the importunate demand for the blue. "They who take the Bath," he told the old Duchess of Marlborough, "shall the sooner have the Garter." He set the example by taking the Bath himself, and became Sir Robert. The following year (1726) he resigned this honour, and became a knight of the higher order.

The fulsome author of the *Night Thoughts* had the previous year received from Walpole a royal pension of two hundred pounds per annum, and he now celebrated the event in his patron's career in some foolish jingle about garter'd sons of praise, our boast of former days, and calling on Britain to see her Walpole shining from afar, his azure Ribbon and his shining Star. It was not a mere poetic figure to call the coveted riband azure; but a few years later it was changed from sky-blue to

the modern garter-blue, in order to distinguish companions of lawful creation from those who had the order
bestowed upon them by the Pretender.   Two points
excited remark in Walpole's case, and they are worth
noticing as signs of the time: one, that he was decorated
for merely civil distinction; the other, that he was a
commoner.   No commoners had been made Knights of
the Garter since Sir Edward Montagu and General
Monk in 1660.   No commoner after Walpole received
the blue riband until Lord North in 1772, and the only
other knights of the order who have sat in the House
of Commons since were Castlereagh and Palmerston.
Queen Victoria desired to give the garter to Sir Robert
Peel in 1845, but Peel, with a characteristic mixture of
shyness and of pride, replied that he sprang from the
people and belonged to the people, and that the honour
would be inappropriate.   We may perhaps wonder that
Walpole did not act on the reason afterwards assigned
by Lord Melbourne for refusing the garter; that he did
not see why he should be such a fool as to buy himself,
when he could buy somebody else with it.   He was
possibly guided as usual by motives of policy.   "Is
ambition imputed to me?" he asked in his great defence
in 1741.   "Why, then, do I still continue a commoner
—I who refused a white staff and a peerage?   I had,
indeed, like to have forgotten the little ornament about
my shoulders, which gentlemen have so repeatedly mentioned in terms of sarcastic obloquy.   But surely though
this may be regarded with envy or indignation in another
place, it cannot be supposed to raise any resentment in
this House, where many may be pleased to see those
honours which their ancestors have worn returned again

to the Commons." Sir Bluestring became the favourite nickname, and the composers of mug-house songs for fifteen years to come found their patrons never tired of listening to choruses of which the point was always the same ; that though the knight had laid down the red riband to take up the blue, a third change awaited him yet, when justice would at last be done by the hempen string at Tyburn.

Tyburn was still a long way off, but the elements of an opposition gradually gathered themselves together. The Tory reaction of Anne was recent, and the state of mind that had made it possible was only quiescent and not extinct. It was Walpole's cue to represent Tory and Jacobite as identical, so as to cover the whole opposition with the taint of disaffection to the revolution settlement and the reigning family. This was no mere manœuvre for party purposes. As Hume shows, cavalier and roundhead, court party and country party, Tory and Whig, all represented genuine divisions of principle in our government ; neither of them disowned either monarchy or liberty, but men of easy temper, attached to peace and order, would lean towards monarchy, while bolder spirits, passionately devoted to liberty, would value the republican part of our mixed scheme. Abstract principles, however, never bring us to sufficiently close quarters in politics. Principles, as Hume excellently says, are changed into affections. Men are guided by what they take to be the balance between advantages and disadvantages. The chief advantage of the Stuart line was its association with stable and ordered public sentiment : its chief disadvantage was its dissidence from the established religion of the people. The great advantage of the Hanoverian line, on the other hand, was its natural favour for that liberty which had raised it to the throne : its great disadvantage lay in the foreign possessions of the Hanoverian princes, which might involve us in the wars and intrigues of continental Europe.[1]

The practical result of Tory prepossessions is shown by Lord-Chancellor Cowper in that remarkable memorial which he laid before George I. on his accession.[2] " Many of the Tories," he says, " would rejoice to see the Pretender restored by a French power, much more if by any safer means ; the best of them would hazard nothing to keep him out, though probably do nothing hazardous to bring him in ; but if ever he should declare himself Protestant, with proper circumstances to make his conversion probable (as, after the death of the French king and his mother, it is not unlikely he may do), they would greedily swallow the cheat, and endeavour by all possible means to put in practice again their old notions of divine, hereditary, and indefeasible right, by a restoration of the person in whom by their opinion that right is lodged." This remained a true description of the equivocal and unstable position of the Tories, for the greater part of Walpole's government. The least Jacobite among them were still very cold friends to the new settlement, and for many years any accident might have turned them into active enemies. These were the group who followed Sir William Wyndham—one of the most respect-

---

[1] *Hume's Essays*, i. 133, and 470 (Green's Edition).

[2] This memorial is printed as an appendix to chapter xvii. of Campbell's *Lives of the Chancellors*; but for some reason has been omitted from later editions.

able figures of his age, notwithstanding the badness of his cause ; a statesman endowed with firmness, dignity, modesty, and the gift, so hard to define but so sensible in operation, of imposing his authority upon his hearers.

The Tories, so early as 1728, were joined by a small group of malcontent Whigs, headed by William Pulteney, who presently became the leader of the coalition against Walpole in the Commons, as Carteret was in the House of Lords. Pulteney left the main body of the Whigs in disgust at not receiving either the office or the confidence to which he justly considered that his talents entitled him. According to one story, Walpole soon discovered that he had made a mistake, and immediately endeavoured to repair it by proposing to make him Secretary of State, but Pulteney's self-love had been too deeply wounded. Another version is, that during the conflict between Townshend and Carteret in 1724, Walpole discovered that Pulteney was intriguing with Carteret, and resolved that as he had chosen to try to gain entrance by that door, the key of the other should be finally turned upon him. Whatever the cause, he went into strong opposition. He was a fine speaker, abounding in sharp epigram and cutting wit, prompt in debate, full of animation and fire, and a master in all the arts of parliamentary attack. But even friendly contemporaries agree that his shining gifts were ruined by uncertainty and instability of mind. "It would be endless," says Chesterfield on one occasion, "to give you an account of the various sallies and extravagances of Pulteney, which change oftener than the wind." Hervey describes him as " vindictive, born with little passions, unequal and uneven, sometimes in very high and sometimes in very low spirits, and full of small enmities." He was so little to be depended on, that the songs represent him as bellowing for liberty to-day, and roaring for power to-morrow, as tight to the Tories at noon, and supping with Whigs at night. He fully deserves Shelburne's remark, that if we examine his long opposition, it will be seen that he never did any good nor attempted to do any. His career was pure faction, and when the hour of triumph arrived, we shall see that he in an instant turned it into the most extraordinary failure in party history.

The secret mover of the machinery of opposition was a wilder and more versatile spirit than any of these, the famous Bolingbroke. We cannot wonder that his own generation should have been dazzled by the genius of a man who had taken the main part in overturning a ministry so covered with glory as that of Marlborough and Godolphin; who showed such unexampled address, alike in framing, carrying, and defending the great instruments of Utrecht; who led men of such force, brilliancy, and position as Carteret, Pulteney, and Wyndham; and who finally, as he had contributed more than any one else to the fall of Marlborough, now boldly applied himself to sap the power of the minister who was as strong and as successful in civil government as Marlborough had ever been in the field.[1] The misanthropy of Swift, the mockery of Voltaire, the sensitiveness of Pope, were all overcome by the fascination of his address, the glitter of his ideas, and the eloquence of his talk, Swift wrote to Stella that Mr. St. John was the greatest young man he ever knew—wit, capacity, beauty, quickness of appre-

---

[1] See Walpole's *George II*, i. 222.

hension, good learning, and excellent taste ; the best
orator in the House of Commons, admirable conversation, good nature, and good manners ; generous and a
despiser of money.[1] Another of his friends vowed, in
a grand transport of praise, that the writings and conversation of Bolingbroke did nothing less than unite the
wisdom of Socrates, the dignity and ease of Pliny, and
the wit of Horace. In every part he was a consummate
posture-master—the stoical philosopher musing on the
true uses of retirement and study, the statesman busily
framing policies, erecting combinations, and moulding
foolish princes into patriot kings, or the simple country
gentleman smoking tobacco with his honest neighbours,
inquiring how the wheat was doing in the four-acre field,
and careful to know the names of all his hounds. Parallels to this extraordinary man have been sought all
through history, from Alcibiades down to Lord Byron ;
he supplied the best poet of his day with philosophy ;
made speeches that intoxicated the House of Commons,
and left such a tradition that illustrious authorities declared that they would rather recover one of Bolingbroke's orations than the lost books of Livy, or " all the
gaps in Greek and Roman lore ; " he developed ideas on
statecraft and the constitution which have lived to find
some favour among eminent men even in our own time ;
and finally, he handled the great and difficult instrument of written language with such freedom and copious-
ness, such vivacity and ease, that in spite of much
literary foppery and falsetto he ranks, in all that
musicians call execution, only below the three or four
highest masters of English prose. Yet of all the char-

[1] 1st November 1711.

acters in our history, Bolingbroke must be pronounced
to be most of a charlatan; of all the writing in our
literature, his is the hollowest, the flashiest, the most
insincere.

Impeached in England he fled to France, entered the
service of the Pretender, and within a year, just as he was
being attainted for high treason at Westminster, he was
at the same time impeached for treason by his new master
at St. Germains. After this unique experience he refreshed
himself by a draught of what he called *consolatio philo-
sophica*, and composed Reflections upon Exile, an edifying collection of platitudes freely borrowed from Seneca.
His sense of the beauties of exile did not prevent him
from abject efforts to bring it to an end. No bankrupt
politician ever surpassed his dissimulation. He hastened
to pay court to Walpole's brother in Paris, entered
into correspondence with the English ministers to the
detriment of his old Jacobite friends, at the same time
intrigued against the English ministers with the French
Government, and finally, after finding out Carteret's intrigues with the Tories, carried their secrets over to the
Whigs. A much more effective step was to bribe the
Duchess of Kendal with a present of eleven thousand
pounds, as the price of his restoration. Walpole was
given to understand that if he did not comply he
would be dismissed, and as a compromise he passed a
bill for the restitution of the family estates, but maintaining the exclusion from Parliament. In his own day,
Walpole was always blamed by his friends for mistaken
lenity in consenting to Bolingbroke's return. According
to the temper of modern times, we are more disposed to
think him weak for not making the amnesty complete.

Bolingbroke's restless ambition, his inveterate love of plots and schemes, his passion for display, were sure to make him the minister's enemy, and his enmity could not have been more injurious in the comparative privacy of the House of Lords, than it proved to be in the pages of the *Craftsman*.   As it was, his vigour, hardihood, and resource made him for ten years the intellectual inspirer of the Opposition both in the press and in Parliament. He had been a Tory highflier, he had been a whimsical, he had been James's Secretary of State; he now became a Whig of the Whigs, denounced legitimacy and legitimists, and, not content modestly to savour the graces of conversion, he insisted on figuring as the only orthodox interpreter of Revolution principles, and with righteous anger branded Walpole for endangering the untold blessings of the Revolution settlement.   Ingenuity was never carried farther than in Bolingbroke's efforts to invent phrases that should catch the followers of Wyndham without startling the friends of Pulteney, and should persuade both that they were engaged in "a virtuous defence of the constitution."   Bolingbroke was not without the dæmonic elements of character : he had fire, energy, penetration, insight, elasticity, fertility, imagination, adventure.   But neither his character nor the flimsy and incongruous creations of his political fancy were calculated to attract the country gentlemen. They keenly relished his attacks on the minister.   They sometimes took his hints about motions and divisions and the mystery of electioneering; but they cared very little about the ideal of a patriot king, and had not the least intention of allowing Prerogative to become the substitute for Influence.   They used his talents, but he

was never either trusted or popular. Wyndham alone
seems to have been warmly and sincerely his friend.
The staunch Jacobites hated him as having betrayed
their master. The honest Whigs hated him as a Tory
renegade. Even the malcontent Whigs suspected and
disliked him. They knew in their hearts that there
was no answer possible to Walpole's scathing description
of him, in one of his most apt and energetic passages, as
ferreting out information for the benefit of foreign am-
bassadors, as making it his trade to betray the secrets
of every court as soon as he left it, as betraying every
master he ever served, as void of all faith and all
honour.[1] In the face of perfidies like these, it is hardly
worth while to dwell on mere inconsistencies in policy :
to note that he who had made peace with France the
keystone of his system, now assailed Walpole for not
being German ; that the minister of Queen Anne who
originated the newspaper stamp, was the loudest champion
of the absolute freedom of the press ; or that the pro-
poser of the first commercial treaty proved the fiercest
opponent of Walpole's move towards free trade. As
might have been expected, he resorted to a common
device of embarrassed politicians ; he called for a national
party. The hypocritical phrase did not make his allies
forget that it was he who had first insisted on drawing
strict party lines and driving the Whigs out of government, any more than it prevented the revival, when power
was once more within reach, of the acutest jealousies
between the two wings of the patriot coalition. " When
I was young," Burke says, " a general fashion told me I
was to admire some of the writings against Sir Robert

[1] Coxe, ch. 42, iii. 148.

Walpole ; a little more maturity taught me as much to despise them." Chatham confessed to the same contempt, though Bolingbroke had been his friend and political coadjutor. The verdict has been confirmed by the judgment of posterity. In vain the consummate artist strives to disguise the shipwrecked adventurer. In vain does he borrow the graces and polish of Plato or Cicero, to turn pamphleteering into philosophy. The flowing rhythm, the impetuosity, the affected union of a student's gravity with the gay breeding of a man of the world, may please the idle ear, but neither in fact nor observation, nor in his own conviction, have his writings foundation or bottom.[1] It seems to be very doubtful whether, even in his own day, either Bolingbroke's writings or his machinations ever did Walpole real damage. It must not be forgotten that after he had been ten years incessantly at work Bolingbroke went back to France (1735), according to some, because Walpole had found him out in treasonable intrigues with a foreign minister ; according to others, because Pulteney plainly told him that "his name and presence in England did hurt." Whatever the reason of his retreat, he went in the mood of a baulked gambler, bitterly disgusted with his confederates, and professing much virtuous surprise at the painful discovery that what they had been aiming at all the time was not the reform of government, but the succession to Walpole ; not a virtuous defence of the constitution, as he had in his

---

[1] Bolingbroke has recently been made the subject of several interesting criticisms, of which the brilliant essay of Mr. Churton Collins and a masterly study by Mr. Harrop are the most important.

innocence been dreaming, but "a dirty intrigue of low ambition."

There was a moment when Walpole seems to have apprehended serious danger from Bolingbroke. The same influences that had forced the minister to assent to his return, were actively at work to procure his admission to power. The matter is very obscure, and perhaps is now hardly worth unravelling, even if it were possible. The authority of the mistress over the king, and the weight of Bolingbroke's bribes with the mistress, were certainly thought by Walpole to constitute a standing peril, and the fluctuations of Hanoverian policy and interest undoubtedly opened a field admirably suited to Bolingbroke's genius for intrigue. He took the bold step of insisting that the king should give his enemy an audience and hear all that he had to say. As might have been expected, mercurial plausibilities were little calculated to move the saturnine mind of the king. "*Bagatelles, bagatelles,*" he answered, when Walpole asked him what Bolingbroke had said. Bolingbroke resembled De Retz in genius for intrigue, though far inferior to him in intrepidity and courage, and so now, just as De Retz, when he found himself repulsed at court, directed all his passion and his hate against Mazarin, Bolingbroke made the destruction of Walpole the object of his life, to be effected by calumny, by wit, by invective and ridicule, by every appeal to the selfishness of bad men and the unguarded prepossessions of the good.

CHAPTER V

THE COURT

AN event now occurred which was by many confidently expected to bring Walpole's career as minister to an end. In the summer of 1727 George I. died on the road to Hanover. The news found Walpole in his rural villa at Chelsea. He instantly rode off to Richmond as fast as he could, to announce to the new king what had happened. The prince always retired to rest after his mid-day dinner, and there Walpole found him. For some time he disbelieved the news, and refused to get out of bed to be told that he was king, as stubbornly as Barnardine in the play refuses Abhorson's summons to rise and be hanged. When he was at length convinced that his father was dead, he dismissed the minister with a curt command to seek Sir Spencer Compton at Chiswick, and from him to take his directions. This was what Walpole had expected. His fidelity to the interests of his former master had apparently ensured the enmity of his successor. As the son hated his father, he could not well love his father's most trusted adviser.

Compton was a younger son of the family of Northampton, and had been Speaker in three Parliaments.

In this capacity he had been successful and popular, and had shown some resource. When a member desired that order might be kept, for he had a right to be heard, the Speaker would make the ingenious rejoinder, " No, sir, you have a right to speak, but the House have a right to judge whether they will hear you." Besides being Speaker, he had been the prince's treasurer ever since his arrival in England. His selection to be the new minister would therefore have been natural ; but the old men were not displaced at once, and before many days were over the king made up his mind not to displace them at all. At the time of the accommodation between the old king and his son, seven years before, Walpole seems to have had as much influence with the Princess of Wales as he ever acquired over her as queen,[1] and the new circumstances may well have revived old impressions.

At first, things at the new court underwent the change of face in which satirists of every age and tongue rejoice. Leicester House, in the old king's lifetime, had been shunned like a city stricken with the plague ; all at once it became thronged from morning to night. Walpole, whose steps had so long been dogged by a mob of toadies and placehunters, now made vacancy wherever he turned. Compton held levées, crowded by men who had sworn in prose and verse that no adverse fate should ever separate them from Sir Robert. The new king's feelings towards the three principal men in his father's government had never been concealed. Walpole he was accustomed freely to describe as rogue and rascal ; the Duke of Newcastle was

[1] Lady Cowper's *Diary*, under date 1720.

an impertinent fool ; and Townshend a choleric blockhead.   Yet the experience of a few days was enough to
show the king that the rascal, the impertinent, and the
blockhead were the three best servants that he was
likely to find.   Compton's incompetency was manifest
within four and twenty hours.   He had, moreover, committed the indiscretion of making the new king's wife
his enemy by paying court to the mistress, and he
was the first to find that the enmity of the new
queen was invariably fatal to its object.   But still
more important causes worked for the retention of the
old ministry.

The most formidable danger to be apprehended, alike
for English and for Hanoverian interests, was any
change in the friendly attitude of France.   Happily
Cardinal Fleury saw no reason why the substitution of
George II for George I. should affect the interests or
policy of France.   He explained his views to Horace
Walpole, the British ambassador : France would hold
firm to all her engagements as one of the allies of
Hanover, if the new king would adhere to the system
of his father, and to the old principle that the common
security of the two countries lay in steadfast union.
Fleury, moreover, sensibly assuring the ambassador that
more would be done in a couple of days of conversation than by volumes of despatches, urged him to repair
at once to London and lay his views before the king.
When Walpole arrived, the king began by scolding him
after his usual manner for quitting his post without
leave.   Then, when the preliminary blustering was over
and the cardinal's letter was produced, King George
was too acute not to see what good news the ambassador

had brought, and at the same time how much easier
it would be to steer the same course if the same ministers remained at the helm.

The delicate operation of fixing the amount of the
civil list turned equally in Walpole's favour. The
Whigs out of place, regarding office as the object of
a party auction, strove to outbid the Whigs in place.
Now this was a sort of play at which Walpole was
not easy to beat. Compton proposed that the queen's
jointure should be settled at 60,000*l.*; Walpole offered
to ask Parliament for 100,000*l.* The grant to the
late king had been 700,000*l.* a year. Walpole gave it to
be understood that he would put it at 800,000*l.*, and
at this sum it was finally settled. The king, in the
conversation with Walpole in which these terms were
discussed, took him by the hand and said, "Consider,
Sir Robert, what makes me easy in this matter will
prove for your ease too; it is for my life it is to be
fixed, and it is for your life."

Before the courtiers could guess what was going
on, Compton had, with tears in his eyes, declared his
incapacity for so arduous a trust, and Walpole and
Townshend were once more reinstalled. As Walpole
drove through St. James's Square, he saw Sir Spencer
Compton's house besieged by people of all ranks eager
to worship the rising sun. "Did you observe," he said
to a friend, "how my house is deserted, and how that
door is crowded with carriages? To-morrow this house
will be deserted, and mine will be more frequented than
ever." Before the secret was out, his wife went to pay
her respects at Leicester House. She could not, says
her son, make her way between the scornful backs and

sharp elbows of the fine people who had a few days before been her steadfast devotees. When the queen called out, "I think I see a friend," and beckoned her forward, everybody eagerly made way; "and as I came back," said Lady Walpole, "I might have walked over their heads if I pleased." It is not surprising that Walpole failed to take exalted views of human nature; at least he had good sense and breadth of mind enough to keep clear of a cheap and shallow misanthropy.

The remarkable woman who now made her first appearance on the stage of great affairs was to play an important part in Walpole's career. Caroline of Anspach came of a branch of the house of Brandenburg. Having lost her father early, the young princess was partially brought up in Berlin. There, in the society of Sophia Charlotte—the friend of Leibnitz and so inquisitively curious that, as Leibnitz said of her, she would know even the why of a why—she acquired that keenness of mind for speculative subjects, and that respect for learning and learned men, which distinguished her from the rest of the gross and unlettered representatives of the Hanoverian stock in England. She possessed by nature the same cheerful, brisk, curious, acute, and stirring character, as both the queen, Sophia Charlotte, and her mother, the old Electress Sophia. She sometimes recalls, too, Charlotte Elizabeth of Bavaria, the niece of the Electress Sophia and cousin therefore of George II, who married the brother of Louis XIV, became the mother of the Regent Orleans, and watched for so many years with shrewd, honest, amazed eyes the strange distractions and devilries of her vile husband and her corrupted son. Queen Caroline's life, like the

lives of these her kinswomen so oddly mated, can
hardly have been a very happy one, if happiness means
the regular satisfaction of our best aims and highest
faculties; but she had that reasonable substitute for
happiness which lies in cheerful stoicism, in an active
constancy of mind, and in a clear-eyed resolution to see
men and things as they are.

George II was always called by his cousin, Frederick
William, the terrible father of Frederick the Great, "My
brother the comedian." He had the strut, the gesticu-
lation, the bustle of the bad play-actor, and, like the bad
actor, he was all the more eager for applause, because he
inwardly suspected that he only half deserved it. He
was not without sterling qualities. He had physical
courage : in Marlborough's wars he had served with
credit ; and even his father, who hated him, admitted
that he fought like a man. He knew how to keep a
secret, and he was proud of being a man of honour and
a man of his word. This did not prevent him from
snatching his father's will from the hands of the Archbishop of Canterbury at his first Council, walking out of
the room with the will in his pocket, and taking care
that it should never be heard of again. He treated the
will of his uncle, the Duke of York, with equally little
ceremony. The shade of George I. could not have complained, for he had burnt both his wife's will and her
father's. Yet George II was rather above than below
the standard of veracity current in his time. When
Hervey observed to Walpole that the king would not
lie, "*Not often*," Walpole replied. He was sober and
temperate in most of his appetites, though not in all ;
and his habits were methodical to a point of mechanical

regularity that drove those who had to live with him almost mad. His drives in the afternoon, his commerce and backgammon at night, his levées and audiences in the morning, were all fixed to the instant, so that as the weary courtiers complained, with an almanack for the day of the week, and a watch for the hour of the day, everybody would know precisely what point in the mill-horse track the court was passing. It was his habit to visit the favourite, Mrs. Howard, every evening in her own apartments at nine o'clock, with such mechanical punctuality that he often walked about his chamber for ten minutes with his watch in his hand, waiting for the blissful moment. A mistake by a valet would throw him into such agitation, that people who came into the room supposed that he must have just received some dreadful piece of news. In ordinary intercourse he was stiff, formal, and uneasy, as men are apt to be who privately doubt their own fitness for a post, but hope that their secret is not found out. He had a laudable impatience with people who did not come quickly to the point; and one of the many reasons why he hated the admission of Pitt to office, was that the great commoner treated him to grand speeches in the closet; they might, he said, be uncommonly fine, but were quite beyond his comprehension. The king's confidence was hard to gain, and he was reserved in showing it, but he was never unstable : he steadily respected the judgment of the queen ; he was firm as a rock for Walpole ; and when the time came, he fought like a lion for Carteret. With all his faults, we must give such a man credit for character. He was avaricious and mean. The only present that he ever made to Walpole was a diamond, and it was found

to be cracked quite through. His temper was passionate
and splenetic, and he was an incessant railer. Though not
exactly bad-hearted or malevolent, he was thoroughly
unfeeling. He is described as timorous in Council.
"He thinks he is devilish stout," said Walpole once,
when the king was bent on going to Hanover, and the
minister was resolved that he should not, "and that he
never gives up his will or his opinion, but he never acts
in anything material but when I have a mind that he
should. Our master, like most people's masters, wishes
himself absolute, and fancies he has courage enough to
attempt making himself so; but if I know anything of
him, he is, with all his personal bravery, as great a
political coward as ever wore a crown."

This was the man whom it was the great business of
the queen's life to humour, to cajole, to amuse, to
restrain, and to lead. She acquired complete ascendancy over him, but it was purchased at a merciless price,
and it needed to be carefully hidden. In spite of his self-
satisfaction the king was too sharp not to know that
every design, project, and combination which he found
in his mind, had been laboriously planted there by
concert between Walpole and the queen. But he
flattered himself that nobody else knew it. To make
the comedy perfect, he was never weary of gibing at
sovereigns who had been governed by women and by
favourites. Charles I. was ruled by his wife, Charles
II by his mistresses, James II by his priests, King
William by his Dutchmen, Queen Anne by Lady Marlborough and Lady Masham. He wound up his list with
a smile of triumph by asking, "And who do they say
governs now ?"

The king had, almost to the end, not only a great
admiration for the queen's judgment, but also, in spite
of his unfaithfulness, a strong attachment to her person.
When he was absent in Hanover, he wrote letters to
the queen thirty pages long, as warm and tender as
those of "a young sailor of twenty to his first mistress."
This did not prevent him from being rough and uncivil,
even when he meant to be kind. One half of his conversation with her was made up of what its unfortunate
victim called snappings and snubbings; and he was in
all circumstances intolerably exacting. He hated the
company of men as much as he delighted in that of
women; and as he could not bear to be alone, the queen
was obliged, for many hours in every day, to watch him
strutting and fuming about her apartment, to listen to
his rude and irascible tirades with affected interest, to
return insults with obsequious flattery, and to practise
all the other slavish artifices by which unlucky women
of sense are so often compelled to manage their tyrants.
His majesty comes into the gallery, snubs the queen,
who happened to be drinking chocolate, for always stuff-
ing; one princess for not hearing him, and another for
being grown fat; one of his sons for standing awkwardly;
Lord Hervey for not knowing what relation the Prince
of Sulzbach was to the Elector Palatine; and then he
carries off the queen to receive more snubs in the
garden. The queen ventures to make some remark to
Hervey about Bishop Hoadley's book on the sacraments.
The king, breaking in, asks her why she loves talking
such nonsense about things she knows nothing about, as
if it were not fools loving to talk of such things, that
made the fools who wrote upon them publish their

nonsense. Then he turns to Hervey and tells him that
if the Bishop of Winchester is his friend, he has a great
puppy and a very dull fellow and a great rascal for his
friend. "It is a very pretty thing for such scoundrels,
when they are raised by favour so much above their
desert, to be talking and writing their stuff, to give
trouble to the government that has showed them that
favour; and very modest in a canting hypocritical knave
to be crying, 'The kingdom of Christ is not of this
world,' at the same time that he as Christ's ambassador
receives six thousand a year." So the torrent of
petulance every day ran on for hour after hour, the
queen all the time, by smiles and nods at the right
places, endeavouring to signify her approval of his
wisdom, to keep herself as safely out of mischief as she
could, and to prevent onlookers from discerning the
depth of her humiliation and chagrin. For an hour or
two before bedtime he would talk about armies or about
genealogies, whilst the queen knitted and yawned.
"She was at least seven or eight hours *tête-à-tête* with the
king every day, during which time she was generally
saying what she did not think, assenting to what she did
not believe, and praising what she did not approve.
She used to give him her opinion as jugglers do a card,
by changing it imperceptibly, and making him believe he
held the same as that he first pitched upon. But that
which made these *tête-à-têtes* seem heaviest was that he
neither liked reading nor being read to (unless it was to
sleep); she was forced like a spider to spin out of her
own bowels all the conversation with which the fly was
taken. For all the tedious hours she spent in watching
him while he slept, or the heavier task of entertaining

him while he was awake, her single consolation was in
reflecting she had power, and that people in coffee-
houses were saying she governed their country, without
knowing how dear the government of it cost her" (*Hervey*).
We may judge how deadly the weariness became from the
story that when Lady Suffolk was falling out of favour,
the Princess Royal actually said that she wished with all
her heart that her father would take somebody else,
"that mamma might be a little relieved from the *ennui*
of seeing him for ever in her room."

No private complaisance was thought by the queen
too hard to be borne, so long as it helped her to retain
exclusive access to the king's ear in public affairs.   No
humiliation was too abject, if she could only restrain
his variable impulses, and guide him along the path that
was indicated by her good Sir Robert.   Walpole often
told her that she was the sole mover of the court, and
that if he could boast of any success in carrying on the
king's affairs, it was all due to her mediation.   "For if,"
he said, "I have had the merit of giving any good advice
to the king, all the merit of making him take it, madam,
is entirely your own, and so much so, that I not only
never did do anything without you, but I know I never
could."   When courtiers heard the queen using meta-
phors about not hanging every hound that ran a little
slower than the rest, provided in the main it kept up with
the pack, they knew very well, and even the king must
have guessed, that the imagery came from Norfolk and
not from Hanover.

Though the king and queen were from their position
the useful guardians of our free constitution, they had
no predilection for political liberty.   The dapper martinet

is said always to have hated his English subjects as
republicans and killers of kings. Even the queen, filled
as she was by the stiff and narrow ideas of German
courts, was never cordially reconciled to the dependence
in which the king was held upon ministers and Parliament. In her heart it was odious to her that the king
should be the pensioner of his people, forced to go to
the House of Commons for every shilling that he needed.
Though she was ready to dispense with ceremony when
it stood in the way of her convenience, as when she
conversed with Lord Hervey for two hours through the
half open door of her bedroom, she always held high
notions of regal etiquette. She sometimes honoured
Sir Robert by dining at his house in Chelsea. The
queen, we are told, sat down to table with Lady
Walpole and any member of the royal family whom
she had brought with her. Sir Robert stood behind
her chair, handed her the first dish, and then retired
into another room, where he dined with the queen's
household attendants. On the other hand, Walpole and
the queen were on terms of familiarity in their discourse
which would now be not only amazing between any
royal consort and a minister, but between any decent
man and any decent woman. It is painful, even at this
distance of time, when they have all shrunk into thin
ghosts and shadows of names, to read some of the jests
with which Walpole regaled the queen, at her own
expense and to her profound secret discomfiture as a
woman.

Much as the queen had to endure in her masculine
desire for power, her use of it was uniformly for good.
She had a thorough grasp of the principles of Walpole's

policy, she comprehended and sympathised with his
temper and his maxims, and she perceived as clearly as
Walpole himself how closely the stability of the dynasty
was bound up with the firm maintenance of a parliamentary constitution. No two personages were ever
more fitted thoroughly to understand one another than
Walpole and Queen Caroline. The queen, however,
had some higher intellectual interests, which to Walpole
probably seemed as pure nonsense as they seemed to
King George. She often tried to make him read Butler's
Analogy, but he told her that his religion was fixed, and
that he had no desire either to change or improve it.
" At no period in the history of our Church," says a
good authority, " has the ecclesiastical patronage of the
Crown been better directed than while it was secretly
dispensed by Queen Caroline ; for a brief period
liberality and cultivation of mind were passports to
promotion in the Church." [1] She offered a bishopric to
Berkeley, and her recommendation led to the preferment
of Butler to Durham. Hoadley was too political and too
liberal in his politics to be a favourite with crowned
heads, but Hare and Sherlock were among her best friends.
Her own theological views undoubtedly leaned to the
latitudinarian, the tolerant, and the heterodox, and
were presumably as empty of spiritual force as the rest
of the rationalism of the time. In her girlhood a
marriage had been projected with the archduke who
afterwards became the Emperor Charles VI, and she
had with that design been instructed in the great con-
troversies between the two creeds, with a view to her
conversion to Romish Church. When the marriage was

[1] Pattison, *Essays*, ii. 109.

abandoned, it was found that instead of preferring either faith to the other, she had learned to suspect both. Her favourite divine was Dr. Samuel Clarke. With him once a week, in the midst of courtiers and fine ladies, she discussed whether the will is free, whether the annihilation of time and space is beyond the power of Omnipotence itself, whether the First Person of the Holy Trinity can annihilate the Second and the Third. Clarke once went with Sir Isaac Newton, to help the great philosopher to explain to her his immortal system. The queen wished to make Clarke a bishop, and employed Walpole to overcome the good man's scruples. The incongruous pair fought the question until the candles were burnt down to the socket; but Walpole found that a metaphysician is not so easily persuaded for his own good as a member of Parliament. According to another story, the queen thought of making Clarke Archbishop of Canterbury, until she was told that he was indeed the most learned and most honest man in the king's dominions, and only in one respect unfit for the see, namely, that he was not a Christian. What is at least as interesting as the queen's correspondence with Leibnitz, or her discrimination in the selection of superior divines,—she was the steady patron of Handel. Even the tranquil atmosphere of art was invaded by the passions of political party, and the court was for Handel because the Prince of Wales was for Bononcini. Handel's noblest work was not produced until after Queen Caroline's death, but she deserves credit for her early recognition of the one resplendent genius who soars above the prosaic level of that uninspired and uninspiring time.

No apology is needed for dwelling at length on the personal character and conduct of the king and queen. To-day the immediate source of a minister's strength is the favour of the House of Commons. In the first half of the eighteenth century the immediate source of strength was the favour of the court. The king was at the mercy of the Whig clans—the Pelhams, the Cavendishes, the Cobhams; but among their representatives he was often able to exercise a limited choice for the first place. He could choose whether the head of the administration should be Sunderland, or Townshend, or Walpole, or Carteret, or Pelham. To this extent the government was the personal government of the king; and the wearisome intrigues that preceded the installation of Walpole, that were always ready to spring up during his supremacy, and that broke out into dire activity immediately after his fall, were the natural results of the king's position as limited arbiter in the personal wrangles of the oligarchy.

Walpole enjoyed the favour of the court because he was able by prudent and skilful management of the House of Commons to obtain supplies, and it was one of his prime maxims both to keep on good terms with the popular House and to exalt its place in the constitution. But it is a great mistake to suppose that Walpole was ever a popular minister. Dr. Johnson once drew a striking and a sound distinction between Walpole's position and that of the first Pitt. Walpole, he said, was a minister given by the king to the people; Pitt was a minister given by the people to the king. This was true and significant. Never at any time did Walpole approach the popularity of the elder Pitt in 1757, of the younger Pitt in 1784, or of Canning in 1827. The same remark has been made of Sir Robert Peel, that not even when he reached the summit of power in 1841 did his fame shine out like that of these three illustrious predecessors. Peel established his power on the confidence of the middle classes, and Walpole undoubtedly in the same way was trusted by the monied interests of his day. But the trust placed in him by the monied interests, and his gradual reconciliation with the landed interest, would have been of no avail without the steady favour of the court.

As it is a mistake to suppose that Walpole ever rode on the flood tide of popularity in its modern sense, so is it a mistake to regard his ascendancy as having been undisputed from the fall of Sunderland. He had loyally shared power with his principal colleague, and it was not until some time after the accession of George II that his supremacy became absolute. Walpole's favour with the queen hastened the rupture between the minister and Lord Townshend. For thirty years they had been intimate friends, and for twenty years out of the thirty they had been close political confederates. They were both strict and constant Whigs. They both suffered the censure of the Tory Parliament of Queen Anne. They acted together in the first administration of George I., and they left it together at the schism from the Sunderland Whigs in 1717. They both rejoined their old colleagues in 1720, and both resumed their old posts in 1721 ; they expected a common disgrace on the accession of George II, and had instead been maintained in their offices as the two pillars of a common policy. All this time Townshend had held the more prominent situation of the two. The Secretary of State was higher in the official ordering than any other political minister. Townshend was a noble, was much the greatest man in his country, and had far the finest house. Walpole was a commoner, had only moderate means, and was for long no higher in station than a score of other Norfolk gentlemen. All this had changed. Walpole had slowly risen by sheer weight of character and ability to be by far the foremost man in the House of Commons. By means of which I shall have something to say later, he had acquired money or credit enough to build himself one of the greatest mansions, not only in Norfolk, but in all England. He had made his eldest son a peer, secured a provision for every member of his family, and decorated himself with a badge that was coveted by kings and princes. The friendship of Queen Caroline now gave him the same pre-eminence in the counsels of the king, as Townshend had in the previous reign enjoyed by his favour with the Duchess of Kendal. This inversion of parts was more than Townshend could bear. His conduct after his fall shows him to have been a really honourable and highminded man, in times when honour and magnanimity were rare among public personages. But he was proud, impetuous, self-confident, very impatient of criticism or contradiction, not persuasive nor lucid in explaining himself, and therefore often heated and passionate, as those who are not lucid are apt to be. He could not endure banter, and Walpole sometimes bantered him even in the royal presence. Finally it was bitter to him to see the decorous hospitalities of Rainham eclipsed by the roystering of Houghton.

Apart from these grounds of personal grudge, the two ministers began to differ in serious things.   Walpole had hitherto contented himself with a general hand in foreign politics.   When Townshend made the Treaty of Hanover, Walpole disapproved of a measure for which he would have to find money, and which he would have against his better judgment to defend in a House of Commons where it was extremely unpopular.   He openly expressed these views, and gave it to be understood that the man who had to devise the means, and to persuade the House to pass the measure, must have a dominant voice in the policy.   With characteristic wisdom he distrusted elaborate schemes of foreign policy, and hated all complicated engagements; Townshend, on the contrary, delighted in them, and the more complicated and entangling they were, the more consummate he thought them.

"As long as the firm was Townshend and Walpole," said Sir Robert in a well-known sentence, "the utmost harmony prevailed; but it no sooner became Walpole and Townshend than things went wrong."   Friendship declined into coolness, and coolness grew to open estrangement.   One evening at Windsor the queen asked the pair where they had dined.   Walpole said that Townshend had dined with a certain elderly lady of quality, of remarkable ugliness, upon whose virtue he could not but think that his lordship had designs. Townshend took fire at the jest, and with a voice shaking with passion, cried out to Walpole, whose own license was notorious and unblushing, "I have not either a constitution that requires such practices, a purse that can support them, or a conscience that can

digest them." Walpole good-naturedly tried to turn
the matter aside, but it needed all the queen's tact to
pacify his angry colleague. On another occasion at
this time, a much more violent altercation took place ;
the two great men seized one another by the collar in a
lady's drawingroom, grasped the hilts of their swords,
and were with much difficulty parted, amid their hostess's
shrill screams for the guard. In 1729 Townshend,
discerning that his position was thoroughly secondary,
gave in his resignation, and retired with dignity and
composure into private life. He never returned to
public affairs. Chesterfield once went to beg him to
come up to the House of Lords, to oppose ministers on
some important business. Townshend replied that he
knew he was extremely warm, his temper and his personal feelings might hurry him into things which in his
cooler moments he should be sorry for, and that he was
irrevocably determined to have no more to do with
public affairs. We can only wonder at the strange
fascination of politics, which has made such honourable
self-command as Townshend's so uncommon among
statesmen whose ambition has missed its mark.

CHAPTER VI

CHARACTERISTICS

RULERS who have gained historic fame by war and
empire, naturally impose heroic and commanding traits
on mankind : rulers who have been great in peace
usually move us by the qualities of a wise and benign
morality.   Sir Robert Walpole's position is in this
respect a peculiar one.   He was a powerful ruler, who
guided the country through a long and profoundly critical ordeal ; yet his name possesses no heroic associations.
He was a great peace minister, yet his career suggests
neither the attractions of private virtue nor the inspira-
tion of lofty public ideals.   It is impossible to make one
of the grand heroic figures of human history out of
nothing more sublime than strong sagacity, penetrating
common-sense, and tenacious public spirit.   Both the
nature of Walpole's task and the characteristics of his
time were fatal to the heroic.   *Quieta non movere* was a
sound and saving maxim for a British minister from the
Peace of Utrecht to the Seven Years' War ; but it is a
maxim without lustre.   Although, however, there is
nothing in such a character as Walpole's to dazzle or to
inspire, he possessed in the highest degree, and displayed
on the widest scale, those qualities of intelligence, prud-

ence, watchfulness, and unshaken constancy, which fit a
man to act a great part in the trying field of civil contention.

The portraits convey no striking impression of character. The glance is firm, but the ruling trait is a some-
what unattractive complacency. Songs and caricatures
abound in references to an everlasting expression between a smile and a sneer. "His face was bronzed over
with a glare of confidence," says his enemy in the *Craftsman*, "an arch malignity leered in his eye." The
malignity is certainly not there, but the confidence is.
In his early days handsome and portly, he grew afterwards to be corpulent and unwieldy, though he rode to
hounds almost to the last.

He was the gayest and easiest of companions. Pope
was the intimate of Bolingbroke, Swift, and others of
Walpole's bitterest foes, and yet he paid to the enemy
of his friends the tribute of those graceful lines—

> " Seen him I have ; but in his happier hour
>   Of social pleasure ill-exchanged for power ;
> Seen him uncumbered with the venal tribe,
>   Smile without art and win without a bribe."

" It would have done you good," his son said, " to hear him
laugh." As another said of him, in an admirable phrase,
" he laughed the heart's laugh." Speaker Onslow said
that his goodness of heart made him the best man to live
with, and to live under, that he ever knew. Pulteney,
who had been his friend and quarrelled with him, and
therefore was inclined to say particularly hard things of
him, declared that Walpole was of a temper so calm and
equal, and so hard to be provoked, that he never felt the
bitterest invectives against him for half an hour. Of Pel-

ham, his pupil and successor, it was said that until he
lost his temper he could never exert his reason. Walpole
was the very opposite. He once lost his temper at a
Cabinet, but he immediately broke up the meeting,
remarking that nobody was fit for business with a
ruffled temper. Even Johnson, who thought that the
first Whig was the Devil, and who always took care in
reporting the parliamentary debates that the Whig dogs
should have the worst of it, still admired Walpole for
his placability, and admitted that he was a fine fellow.

A contemporary story gives a singular glimpse of the
easy terms on which Walpole stood with men who every
day denounced him as the vilest of wretches. Pulteney,
though he had seceded from the regulars of his party,
supposed, childishly enough, that the virtue of Whig
principles would remain in him if he continued to sit on
Whig benches. One day,

> " Mr. Pulteney, sitting upon the same bench with Sir
> Robert Walpole in the House of Commons, said : ' Sir Robert,
> I have a favour to ask of you.' ' O, my good friend Pul-
> teney,' said Sir Robert, ' what favour can you have to ask of
> me ? ' ' It is,' said Mr. Pulteney, ' that Dr. Pearce may not
> suffer in his preferment for being my friend.' ' I promise
> you,' returned Sir Robert, ' that he shall not.' ' Why, then,
> I hope,' said Mr. Pulteney, ' that you will give him the
> deanery of Wells.' ' No,' replied Sir Robert, ' I cannot
> promise you that for him, for it is already promised.' " [1]

Walpole gave Pulteney's friend another deanery, and
Pulteney, thinking gratitude for private favours a higher
virtue than regard for the public weal, wrote to the new
dean to vote for Sir Robert's man if there should

---

[1] Coxe, ch. 39, iii. 46.

be a contest at Winchester.[1] The bonhomie of the House of Commons is very superficial, and there was nothing to prevent Pulteney, after writing to his dean, from fulminating against the enormities of Walpole in buying votes by conferring places.

buying votes

Like his father before him, Walpole was a lover of company. There are few more curious pictures of conviviality under difficulties than that of George I., after a morning's hunting at Richmond, drinking punch and talking dog Latin with Walpole all the afternoon. The minister was not a drunkard, as Harley, Carteret, and Daniel Pulteney all were. Though he probably consumed a quantity that in modern opinion would constitute a hard drinker, he was too laborious and systematic a worker all his life to have been habitually addicted to gross excess. The vast augmentation of public business since his day, due to extension of dominion, to immense increase of population, to rapidity and multiplicity of communications, to the vigilance of the newspapers, and to the boundless activity and exactingness of a reformed House of Commons, has doubtless made a great difference in the weight of ministerial burdens. Still there will always be industrious ministers and lazy ministers, whether the work of the department be heavy or light; and Walpole was one of the most industrious ministers that ever sat in Downing Street.[2] Some of his industry

---

[1] Quoted from Pearce by Coxe, ch. xxxix. iii. 46.

[2] At this time the house, which is now No. 10 Downing Street, was then the only official residence in that famous purlieu. It belonged to the Crown, and Bothmar, the Hanoverian Minister, lived in it. When Bothmar died, George II wished to make Walpole a present of it. Walpole refused it as a personal gift, and they agreed that it should for the future always go with the offices of First Lord of the Treasury and Chancellor of the Exchequer.

was such as few men of business would now regard as
sensible.   According to Coxe, he seldom employed a
secretary.   Every letter of his that has been found was
wholly written in his own hand ; and it is believed that
the copies in the Hardwicke collection were taken from
originals all in his own writing.   He even underwent the
slavery of transcribing whole letters from other people,
and we are assured that the family papers abounded with
extracts from dispatches, and memoranda upon them,
which prove his indefatigable exertions.   He always
thought for himself, and never fell into the too common
weakness of allowing subordinates in the office to think
for him.   He never meddled with the business of others,
and never allowed others to do his own.   Like most,
though not quite all great workers, he was both rapid
and methodical.   He was contrasted by contemporaries
with the Duke of Newcastle.   The duke was all hurry
and confusion, while Sir Robert, who had ten times the
amount of business, was never in a hurry.   "He did
everything with the same ease and tranquillity as if he
was doing nothing."

Walpole was none the less devoted in his application
to serious affairs for being a keen sportsman.   George II
expressed his contempt for men of quality who spent
their time in tormenting a poor fox, that was generally a
much better beast than any of those that pursued him,
inasmuch as the fox hurts no other animal but for his
subsistence, while those brutes who hurt him did it only
for the pleasure of hurting.   But he forgave Walpole
for this obnoxious relaxation, because all the other eleven
months of the year he gave up to the business of his
prince.   Besides his sport in Norfolk, Walpole hunted

with a pack of beagles in Richmond Park; and it is said
of him, as it is of Lord Althorp, that when the letters
arrived he first opened that from his gamekeeper. It
needs not to be added of such a man, that he was a great
sleeper. "I put off my cares," he said, "when I put off
my clothes."

Walpole's faults of external demeanour were of a
kind of which our own age has become intolerant. His
talk at table was such as to-day would send all the
ladies flying from the room. He had that very sorry
vice which Chesterfield calls his desire to be thought to
have a polite and happy turn for gallantry, and he
boasted of his successes with a coarseness that would
now cause instant expulsion from the mess of any garrison
or any circuit in Great Britain. His extraordinary laxity
in this part of private morality reached to so incredible
a pitch, that he seems to have been indifferent to the
doubtful fidelity of his own wife, and to the legitimacy of
his eldest son's eldest boy, though the boy was heir to
the Walpole peerage.

Ceremonious people complained of a want of dignity
in Walpole's manners; it was the natural consequence of
the want of moral dignity in his character. Policy may
have had a share in it. A hearty kind of frankness,
which sometimes seemed impudence, says Chesterfield,
made the world think that he let them into his secrets,
while the impoliteness of his manners seemed to show his
sincerity. Though he was boisterous in his ways, and
though he appears never to have lost his Norfolk accent,
it is caricature to compare him with the Westerns and
Topehalls of the day. It is true that Walpole was no
scholar and no reader. "I wish I took as much

delight in reading as you do," he said to a friend after his retirement, "it would be the means of alleviating many tedious hours; but, to my misfortune, I derive no pleasure from such pursuits." Yet there was nothing illiterate or uneducated about his speeches. The standard books contain passages from his great speech on the Peerage Bill; they are as far as possible from the vein of Squire Western. Onslow says that this performance had as much eloquence and genius in it, as had ever up to that time been heard in Parliament. The speech on the Triennial Bill (1734) is a masterpiece of ready invective and of argument. Chatham declared that the attack on Wyndham on the occasion of the secession (1740) was one of the finest speeches he ever heard. Hervey's report of Walpole's address to his political friends on the withdrawal of the excise scheme, shows it to have had not only animation and energy, but dignity. His political pamphlets are clear and straightforward statements in sound English. His reported conversations, and some of his private correspondence, show Walpole to have had both neatness and facility in the trick of Latin quotation. It is true that in one of the best known parliamentary anecdotes of the time, he once lost a guinea by a blunder in a very familiar verse. He quoted Horace's line as

"Nil conscire sibi, nulli pallescere culpæ."

Pulteney replied that his Latin was as bad as his logic, and that the right words were *nulla pallescere culpa.* Walpole offered to bet him a guinea. The clerk at the table gave it against the minister, who threw the guinea down. Pulteney, catching it, held it up to the House, calling out, "'Tis the first money I've had from the

Treasury these many years, and it will be the last." The error was no worse than Burke's false quantity when he cried, *magnum vectigal est parcimonia.* Yet Burke was not illiterate.

Like other charges against Walpole, his offence in shutting the door of patronage in the face of genius has been made far too much of. We have already seen that he procured two hundred pounds a year to the author of the *Night Thoughts.* He offered a pension to Pope, who declined on the ground that he never thought himself so warm in any party's cause as to deserve their money. He subscribed for ten copies of Fielding's works in 1743, though Fielding had abused him. He sent the unfortunate Savage bank notes. He insisted that Prior, Steele, and Addison had all shown that the most accomplished men of letters make the worst men in affairs; but to please a friend he made Congreve a Commissioner of Customs, predicting, however, that they would find he had no head for business. It is true that he disappointed the expectations of Swift, and thereby incurred the formidable enmity of that powerful genius; but I see no reason why we should condemn Walpole for leaving the unhappy man at "wretched Dublin in miserable Ireland." [1] It is true that he looked upon writing as a mechanical business, and "took up with any pen that he could find in public offices"; but Walpole might well think that when the hack pamphleteer had pocketed his guineas, all the honour had been paid that such literature as his deserved.

He cared little more for musicians than he cared for literature, calling them a pack of fiddlers. For pictures he

---

[1] Swift, xvii. 17.

had both a genuine enthusiasm and a good judgment.
Many of the noble houses in Rome, Florence, and Venice
were selling their pictures, and Walpole bought some of
the best of them. Even in the most anxious days of
1742 he took the keenest interest in a Domenichino,
which was too long on its way to England, and after
his fall he alarmed his son by proposing a jaunt to
Bologna, Florence, and Rome to see the galleries. His
collection, or most of it, afterwards found its way to St.
Petersburg, when Walpole's grandson was driven to raise
money on the treasures of his ancestors, like the Zambe-
carri and Pallavicini before him.

Lord Campbell whimsically complains that Walpole
is responsible, by his utter neglect of literature and
literary men, for giving to official life in England that
" aristocratic feeling and vulgar business-like tone which
it has ever since retained." As if there were any relation between the cause and its alleged effect. Nobody
did less for men of letters than the younger Pitt, yet no
minister ever held, in transacting public business, a loftier
or less vulgar tone. As for Walpole infecting public life
with aristocratic feeling, it is worth remembering that he
belonged to no great family, and formed no powerful con-
nections. When men talk of the Venetian oligarchy of
patrician Whigs, they forget that the patrician oligarchy
was controlled in its palmiest days by a plain country
gentleman. This was one of the taunts most constantly
flung at him by his enemies, as it was a source of just
pride to his own family. Walpole's feeling, in truth, was
much less aristocratic than it was bourgeois. This was
evident long before he reached the summit of his power.
It would have been a graceful decoration to his solid

gifts if Walpole had played the patron of art and letters ;
but after all the work of government is the dispatch of
business, and it is childish to quarrel with a statesman
for giving to it a business-like tone.   We may wish that
Walpole had lighted up his speeches and his policy with
the language of an elevated imagination. Still, as his son
truly said, his eloquence was made for use. He had
a melodious voice and little gesture, and is described
by contemporaries as an artful rather than an eloquent
speaker, fluent, ready, and vigorous in reply, with great
skill in catching the humour of the House, and singular
clearness in unfolding intricate matters, making people
think that they understood when they did not.   He
was right in leaving the declamations of Pitt un-
answered, and in thinking that he had done enough
when he had met the homely contentions of Sir John
Barnard.   A solid reply to a solid argument was worth
a whole library of flashy classical references, delusive
historical parallels, and all the rest of the elegant clap-
trap which Bolingbroke absurdly called the philosophy
of history.   The first qualification in one who aspires
to a ruling place in the counsels of a nation is, that
he should have sound and penetrating judgment; the
second is ample and accurate knowledge of the business in hand; and the third is tenacity of will and
strength of character.   All this is the very root of
the matter, and the root of the matter Walpole had.
The arts of management were a useful, perhaps an
indispensable, adjunct.   Nevertheless, it was not the
arts of management alone or even principally,—it was
his practical grasp of the facts of public business,—
that enabled Walpole to acquire at the same time favour

in the closet of the king, unbounded influence in the
House of Commons, and great, though unhappily not
always unbounded, authority over public opinion in the
country.

Burke rightly contends that Walpole's faults were
superficial. " A careless, coarse, and over-familiar style
of discourse, without sufficient regard to persons or occasions, and an almost total want of political decorum,
were the errors by which he was most hurt in public
opinion." It is certainly a mistake to dismiss Walpole
as a pure cynic. He laughed at the patriotic professions
of his opponents, but then they deserved no better. He
refused to expect too much from men, but this is a virtue,
and not a vice, in one who has to govern men as they
are, and not as the moralist nobly strives to make them.
Government, like all the practical arts, means the over-
coming of difficulties. It is the greatest of the practical
arts, because its ends are the highest, and the difficulties
the most subtle, complex, and incalculable. The world
will never place Walpole in the highest rank among
those who have governed men, for in the world's final
estimate character goes farther than act, imagination
than utility, and its leaders strike us as much by what
they were as by what they did. But Walpole was high
enough for his task ; he possessed the qualities and
mastered the maxims that it required. There are
few difficulties, Walpole said in his letters to Pelham
after his own career was closed, "that cannot be surmounted, if properly· and resolutely engaged in. . . .
It is a pity that you have not time, for time and
address have often carried things that met at the
first onset with great reluctance." He was told

that somebody had deserted to the Tories after
promising that he would always stand by the
Whigs. "I advise my young men," Walpole said,
"never to use *always*." He had the true political tem-
perament, which makes it possible for a man to be at
once intrepid and circumspect. No statesman ever adhered more consistently to all the great articles of his
creed; but, as Hervey says, "he had been too long
conversant in business not to know that in the fluctua-
tion of human affairs and variety of accidents to which
the best concerted schemes are liable, they must often
be disappointed who build on the certainty of the most
probable events; and therefore seldom turned his
thoughts to the provisional warding off future evils which
might or might not happen; or the scheming of remote
advantages, subject to so many intervening crosses; but
always applied himself to the present occurrence, studying
and generally hitting upon the properest method to
improve what was favourable, and the best expedient
to extricate himself out of what was difficult." Satisfied that he was striving for some broad and honest end,
he was not always rigorous as to means. "*He durst do
right*," says his son, "*but he durst do wrong too*." Grave and
many are the dangers of the courage to do wrong; yet,
on the whole, Walpole must be pronounced to have got
discredit for more wrong than he ever did.

The accusation that Walpole was intensely wedded to
power, is so little grave as hardly to be an accusation at
all. Any man with conscious faculty of strength, and a
love of the active business of government, is naturally
wedded to power. It may be said that Fox and Burke
were strong men, and yet were free from the covetous-

ness of office that consumed men like Walpole and like
Pitt.   But neither Fox nor Burke ever showed that
he possessed remarkable aptitude for carrying on public
business; they were for much too short a time in office
to acquire the habit and the passion for it; and they
were never led into temptation by having any real
chance of seizing power, after Mr. Pitt once rose above
the horizon.   A man may be a resplendent rhetorician
like Burke, or he may have commanding views on politics
like Fox, without being eager for personal power; but as
a rule a practical statesman, conscious of ability for a
ruling part in large public transactions, will be as fond of
power as Walpole was or as Pitt.   Walpole, moreover,
like most great ministers, identified his own personality
with high objects of national policy; private triumphs
were never separated in his mind from the success of
public causes; and he insisted on having power, because
he was convinced that he knew how to use it well.   But
bad or feeble men, it may be argued, often think the
same.   The Duke of Newcastle was in his own particular
way as fond of power as Walpole.   This only shows that
the love of power is in itself neither a virtue nor a vice.
"My Lord," said Chatham to the Duke of Devonshire,
"I am sure that I can save this country, and that nobody else can."   There are times when it is a statesman's
duty to insist upon power.   The only question with
which history needs to concern itself is not whether
Walpole was intensely wedded to power, but whether
his possession and use of it were important for the
public good.

Then is it true to say that Walpole was unscrupulous
in his means for grasping power and keeping it ?   That

he gave some advice without a blush which any leading
English statesman to-day would readily rather extinguish
his public life than give, is unfortunately too certain.
Writers on morals tell us that conduct has an æsthetic
and an ethical aspect; it is beautiful or ugly, as well as
right or wrong.   Walpole's counsels to Queen Caroline,
and after her death to the king's own daughters, were
indecorous and disgusting, apart from their immorality.
It is certain, too, that, as some say, he had not the
delicate sense of honour which marks the ideal public
man.   But it cannot be disguised that many men have
shown a want of a fine sense of honour, whom still
we should hesitate to brand generally as either unscrupulous or unprincipled.   Chatham acted in a way
that was not at all to his honour, when he first offered
to screen Walpole, and then on his offer being repulsed,
redoubled the violence of his attack.   George III did
many shabby, cunning, and unscrupulous things, yet
tradition is gradually coming to pass him off as a very
honest gentleman.   Did Mr. Pitt exhibit perfect delicacy
of honour when, on coming back to power in 1804, he
allowed the stubborn king to ostracise Mr. Fox?   Yet
Pitt is usually treated as the pink of moral elevation, and
he did undoubtedly take a loftier view of the connection
between public authority and private honour than had
been the fashion before his time.   The equity of history
requires that we shall judge men of action by the standards
of men of action.   Nobody would single out highminded-
ness as one of Walpole's conspicuous attributes.   It is
not a very common attribute among active politicians in
any age.   On the other hand, Walpole was neither low-
minded nor small-minded.   His son had a right to boast

that he never gave up the interests of his party to serve
his own, though he often gave up his own opinions to
please friends who were serving themselves.   With the
firmest confidence in himself, he was neither pragmatical
nor arrogant.   He was wholly free from spite and from
envy ; he bore no malice, though when he had once
found a man out in playing tricks, he took care never to
forget it ; and he was right, for the issues at stake were
too important to allow him to forget.

It is said that he could not brook a colleague of
superior ability, and that he took care to surround himself with mediocrities like the Duke of Newcastle.   We
may test the accusation by the conduct of Chatham.
Nobody has ever taunted him with this ignoble jealousy,
yet he acted precisely as Walpole acted.   After fighting
against Newcastle as long as he could, he gave way to
him just as Walpole had found it expedient to do.   " I
borrowed the Duke of Newcastle's majority," said Pitt
in 1757, "to carry on the public business."   It was his
majority, not his mediocrity, that Walpole valued.   So
with the proscriptions.   Pitt peremptorily excluded
Henry Fox from his famous administration, though Fox
was the ablest debater in Parliament ; and he declined
to advance Charles Townshend, who was more near to
being his intellectual equal than anybody else then in
the House of Commons.   Neither in Pitt's case nor
Walpole's case is it necessary to ascribe their action to
anything worse than the highly judicious conviction
that whether in carrying out a great policy of peace like
Walpole's, or an arduous policy of war like Pitt's, the very
worst impediment that a minister can have is a colleague
in his cabinet who spoils superior ability by perversities

of restlessness and egotism. There is not one of the able men ostracised, as it is called, by Walpole, whose political steadiness and personal fidelity he could safely trust; and not one of them, let us not forget to add, who, for fifteen years after his fall, ever showed himself any better able to work with other colleagues and leaders, than he had been to work with Walpole.

Walpole took the pleasures, the honours, the prizes of the world as they came in his way, and he thoroughly relished and enjoyed them; but what his heart was seriously set upon all the time—seriously, persistently, strenuously, devotedly — was the promotion of good government and the frustration and confusion of its enemies. When men got in his way, he thrust them aside, without misgiving or remorse, just as a commander in the field would remove a meddling, wrongheaded, or incompetent general of division without remorse. But to be remorseless is a very different thing from being unscrupulous. I am not aware of a single proof that Walpole ever began those intrigues against his enemies, which they were always so ready to practise against him. It was Stanhope and Sunderland, not Walpole, who began and carried out the intrigues that ended in the schism of 1717. It was Carteret who caballed with the Tory leaders against his own colleagues after Sunderland's death. It was Bolingbroke and the Duchess of Kendal who strove by underhand arts to procure access for the former to George I., and when Walpole found out what was going on, he at once boldly urged the king to grant Bolingbroke his audience, and to hear all that he had to say. It was Chesterfield who tried to set up a clique against Walpole within

his own ministry.   Much is made of the case of
Townshend.   But it is rather a paradox to prove Walpole's imperious refusal to share power with able colleagues by referring us to Townshend, with whom he
worked in unbroken cordiality for the best part of thirty
years, and with whom he did loyally share power, himself in a relation rather subordinate than otherwise, for
ten of these years.   It was Townshend, moreover, who
at the last took advantage of his journey with the king
to Hanover, secretly to ingratiate himself in the royal
favour to the disadvantage of Walpole at home.   Plenty
of intriguing was carried on, but not by Walpole.   A
candid and particular examination of the political history
of that time, so far as the circumstances are known to
us, leads to the conclusion that of all his contemporaries,
from men of genius like Bolingbroke and Carteret, from
able and brilliant men like Townshend and Chesterfield,
Wyndham and Pulteney, down to a mediocre personage like the Duke of Newcastle, Walpole was the
least unscrupulous of the men of that time, the most
straightforward, bold, and open, and the least addicted
to scheming and cabal.   He relied more than they did,
not less, upon what after all in every age is the only
solid foundation of political power, though it may not
always lead to the longest terms of office—upon his own
superior capacity, more constant principle, firmer will,
and clearer vision.

That Walpole practised what would now be regarded as parliamentary corruption is undeniable.   But
political conduct must be judged in the light of political
history.   Not very many years before Walpole, a man
was expected to pay some thousands of pounds for

being made Secretary of State, just as down to our own time he paid for being made colonel of a regiment. Many years after Walpole, Lord North used to job the loans, and it was not until the younger Pitt set a loftier example that any minister saw the least harm in keeping a portion of a public loan in his own hands for distribution among his private friends. For a minister to buy the vote of a member of Parliament was not then thought much more shameful, than almost down to our own time it has been thought shameful for a member of Parliament to buy the vote of an elector. Is it a greater sin against political purity to give a member five hundred pounds for his vote, than to advance three thousand for the purchase of his seat ? Yet even the austere Pitt laughed, as Walpole might have laughed, at what he called the squeamish and maiden coyness of the House of Commons, in hesitating to admit the right of the owners of rotten boroughs to be compensated for the disfranchisement of their property. It is absurd to suppose that Walpole first tempted mankind into rapacity and selfishness. Even his enemies admitted that corruption had been gaining ground ever since the time of Charles II. Nobody denies that in all its forms, the venality alike of members and of constituencies was vastly worse thirty years after Walpole's disappearance, than anybody ever asserted it to be in his time. To say, with some modern writers, that Walpole organised corruption as a system, that he made corruption the normal process of parliamentary government, that he governed by means of an assembly which was saturated with corruption, is to use language enormously in excess of any producible evidence and of all legiti-

mate inference. It is to attach a weight to the furious
and envenomed diatribes of the *Craftsman*, to which
the very violence of their language shows them not to
be entitled. With unanswerable force it has been asked
by Sir Robert Peel and other men of experience in
public affairs, how it came about that if Walpole did
really corrupt his age, and if the foundation of his
strength was the systematic misapplication of the public
money to the purposes of bribery, yet a Select Committee
of twenty-one members — nineteen of them his bitter
enemies—appointed after his fall to lay a siege to his
past life equal in duration to the siege of Troy, produced
no specific facts to support the allegations of bribery
which had been used every week and every day for so
many years to inflame public resentment against him?
Two of the great heads of accusation shrunk up to
miserable dimensions, and the third remained a matter
of vague and unsupported inference. Would so lame
and impotent a conclusion have been possible if substantial grounds for the accusation had been in existence?

The charge of under influence at elections ended in
the production of a mere mouse from the labouring
mountain. Walpole appears to have promised the mayor
a place in the revenue service at Weymouth, in order to
secure a returning officer of the right colour; to have
removed some customs officers who declined to vote for
the right candidate ; and to have disbursed some petty
sums for legal proceedings in boroughs. We find
nothing like the lavish purchase of boroughs that was
practised wholesale by George III, and which explains
the vast debts that loaded the civil list of a king who
was personally the most frugal of men. Lord North

thought nothing of paying Lord Edgcumbe fifteen
thousand pounds for his boroughs, or buying three seats
from Lord Falmouth for seven thousand five hundred
pounds, though the bargain nearly went off because he
would not make the pounds guineas.[1] Walpole never
approached such a scale as this.

Nor, again, did the article of conceding fraudulent
contracts produce any more appalling disclosure than
that in the single case of a not very large contract for
payment of troops in Jamaica, the terms had been
suspiciously handsome. Finally, the grand accusation of
peculation and profusion in the expenditure of the
secret service money can be placed no higher than a
doubtful inference from a doubtful figure. The committee founded their case on the amount of the secret
service money. That amount they pronounced to be so
excessive that it could only be explained by a corrupt
and improper destination. They took a period for the
purposes of comparison, at their own will and pleasure.
The secret service money during the ten years from
1707 to 1717 only amounted to three hundred and
thirty-eight thousand pounds. The same head under
Walpole's administration from 1731 to 1741 was no less
than one million four hundred and forty thousand
pounds. Therefore, they argued—and modern writers
are content with their argument—a large proportion of
the immense expenditure of secret service money in
Walpole's government was devoted to the direct pur-

---

[1] See the *Abergavenny Papers*, printed by the Historical Manu-
script Commission. I believe the unprinted portions of the correspondence between George III and Robinson contain still more
astonishing examples of the scale on which the royal boroughmonger
went to work.

chase of members of Parliament.   The premiss, we
repeat, can only be accepted with qualifications; next,
even if the premiss be taken as offering a precisely
just and accurate comparison, the desired conclusion
does not necessarily or even reasonably follow from it.[1]
The ten years from 1707 to 1717 were arbitrarily
chosen; if the first ten years of Anne or of George I.
had been taken, the figure would have been much
higher, and therefore more favourable to Walpole.   The
items of the account, moreover, are taken in one way, in
order to attenuate the figure of the first period, and in
another way, when the object is to expand the figure of
the second period; certain payments were charged to
the secret service fund in one case, which in the other
case had either not been made, or else had gone to
another account.   The comparative statement is therefore fallacious.   Fairly measured, this branch of expenditure, so far as it covered a really secret employment
of money which it would be against the interest of the
public service to disclose, amounted during ten years of
Walpole's administration to less than an annual average
of seventy-nine thousand pounds; and that, according to
Coxe, is much less than the sum expended for similar purposes during a similar term of years before the revolution.

Let us, however, suppose that the amount was even
higher than this.   Why are we to assume as a matter
of course that most of it was spent in buying members
or boroughs, rather than in the avowed objects of
buying secret intelligence both at home and from
abroad, and in buying foreign ministers?   It is certain

[1] The reader will find the matter elaborately examined by Coxe
in his sixty-first chapter.

that Walpole was always singularly well informed as
to the designs of foreign courts.   There were also people
at home on whom it was necessary to keep a still
more vigilant eye.   The designs of Jacobite plotters
were obscurer and more intricate than the diplomatic
manœuvres of Madrid, Vienna, or Versailles.   Walpole
was wisely willing to pay handsomely for good information about them.   It was said of him that while he was
profuse to his friends, his liberality was literally unbounded to his tools and his spies.   Even in our day,
no British. minister has ventured to dispense with
services of this odious kind, and every minister still
very properly refuses to account to Parliament or to any
auditor for a shilling of it.   That some of this money
went in bribes to members of Parliament, it would be
childish to deny.   We shall presently come upon an
instance where nine hundred pounds was paid to two
members of the House of Commons for their support,
(below, p. 195).   Let us take that as incontrovertible.
But it goes a very little way towards the broad accusation that we are examining.   The very fact that the
king grumbled loudly at a transaction which cost no
more than nine hundred pounds, shows that such transactions did not usually mount up to a very large proportion of one hundred and forty-four thousand pounds a
year.   The one detailed case, therefore, that can be
adduced to support the assumption that most of the
secret service money at Walpole's disposal went in
parliamentary corruption, itself shows that the assumption is altogether exaggerated and extravagant.   The
figures prove too much.   We may admit that the
gentlemen who had taken Walpole's money would be

likely to hold their peace about it, and we know that those who paid the money were authorised by the king to refuse to give evidence. Yet when all allowance has been made for these facts, considering how many scores of men must have been concerned, what enormous sums on the hypothesis must have passed, and how passionately ready the great majority of the committee were to procure evidence good or bad at any price, it is surely incredible that, if corruption had been practised on anything approaching to the vast and systematic scale which is so loosely imputed, not one single case should have been forthcoming.

The substance of the charge of corruption is to be sought, not in occasional payment of blackmail to a member or a patron, but in the fact that he reserved the Crown patronage, down to the last morsel, exclusively for members of his own party. He acted on the principle that is accepted in the United States, that is not disavowed in France, and that, although disavowed in Great Britain, has not even yet wholly disappeared there. A member of Parliament who desired anything, from a lucrative office for himself down to a place as tide-waiter for the son of a tenant, knew that his only chance would be to support the administration. The number of offices held by men in Parliament was very great. When Burke introduced his famous scheme of economical reform (1780), he boasted that it would destroy influence equal to the offices of at least fifty members of Parliament. In Walpole's time the number of place-holders at the pleasure of the Court must have been considerably in excess of fifty; for the place-bill of 1743 had excluded a certain number of subordinate personages from seats in Parliament. Walpole insisted that all these gentlemen should be sound Whigs. To that extent, acting especially on the owners of boroughs, he systematically affected the disinterestedness and independence of the House of Commons.

Walpole has no doubt suffered much in the opinion of posterity, as the supposed author of the shallow and cynical apophthegm, that "*every man has his price.*" People who know nothing else about Walpole, believe and repeat this about him. Yet the story is a pure piece of misrepresentation. He never delivered himself of that famous slander on mankind. One day, mocking the flowery and declamatory professions of some of the patriots in opposition, he insisted on finding self-interest or family interest at the bottom of their fine things. "*All these men,*" he said, "*have their price.*" "As to the revolters," he told the king, "I know the reasons and I know the price of every one of them." Nor was he wrong, as time showed. It was not a general but a particular proposition, and as a particular proposition it was true. When an honest man came in his way, Walpole knew him well enough. "I will not say," he observed, "who is corrupt, but I will say who is not, and that is Shippen." And yet "honest Shippen" was one of the stoutest of his opponents.

The absence of any tangible evidence of novel, extraordinary, lavish, and widespread parliamentary corruption on Walpole's part, only coincides with the best positive testimony that we can get. Pitt, who was one of the most vehement promoters of the Secret Committee, five years later publicly acquitted Walpole of the worst of the charges brought against him, in

terms ample enough to satisfy the late minister's own
sons.[1]   Burke, again, says that it was his fortune to converse with many of the principal actors against Walpole,
and to examine with care original documents concerning
important transactions of those times (*Regicide Peace*, i.)
His writings, as everybody knows, contain more than one
passage showing that he had informed himself about Walpole's character and acts ; and in truth much of the great
writer's theoretic wisdom is but the splendid generalisa-
tion of the great minister's particular policy and practice.
What Burke has to say on the point that we are now
discussing is this :—" Walpole was an honourable man
and a sound Whig.   He was not, as the Jacobites and
discontented Whigs of his own time have represented
him, and as ill-informed people still represent him, a
prodigal and corrupt minister.   They charged him, in
their libels and seditious conversations, as having first
reduced corruption to a system.   Such was their cant.
But he was far from governing by corruption.   He
governed by party attachments.   The charge of systematic corruption is less applicable to him, perhaps,
than to any minister who ever served the crown for
so great a length of time.   He gained over very few
from the opposition."—(*Appeal from New to Old Whigs*).
Evidence of this kind, coming from a man of affairs in
the generation immediately following, in contact with
some actors in those events and with many who must
have known about them at first hand, must outweigh
any amount of sweeping presumptions by historians
writing a century and a half after Walpole's fall.   The
part and proportion of corruption in Walpole's manage-

---

[1] Horace Walpole to Mann, 23d February 1747, ii. 74.

ment of members is to be gathered from what he did to secure the rejection of the bill for lowering the interest on the funds. He got time enough, says Hervey, "to go about to talk to people, to solicit, to intimidate, to argue, to persuade, and perhaps to bribe." This may be taken as a fair example of his usual practice. Bribery was an expedient in the last resort, and the appeal to cupidity came after appeals to friendship, to fear, to reason, and to all those mixed motives, creditable, permissible, and equivocal, which guide votes in reformed and unreformed parliaments alike.

The pecuniary affairs of public men are no concern of the outside world, unless they are tainted with improbity. So many charges were made against Walpole under this head, that it is necessary to glance at them. I shall begin with the least serious. Very early in his career of minister Walpole was taunted with abusing his patronage by granting places and reversions of places to his relatives. When his son Horace was little more than a child, he was made Clerk of the Estreats and Controller of the Pipe, with a salary of three hundred pounds a year. At the age of eighteen or nineteen, he became Inspector of Customs; on resigning that post a year later, he was made Usher of the Exchequer, then worth nine hundred pounds a year; and Horace Walpole was able to boast that from the age of twenty he was no charge to his family. The duty of the Usher was to furnish paper, pens, ink, wax, sand, tape, penknives, scissors, and parchment to the exchequer, and the profits rose from nine hundred pounds a year to an average of double that amount. The post of Collector of the Customs, worth nearly two thousand pounds a year, was

granted to Walpole himself, and for the lives of Robert
and Edward his sons. The bulk of the proceeds of this
patent he devised to his son Horace. In 1721 the minister
made his eldest son Clerk of the Pells, with three thousand
a year; and in 1739 he gave him the gigantic prize of
Auditor of the Exchequer, with a salary of seven
thousand pounds. Then when the eldest son resigned
the Pells on receiving the Auditorship, the Pells and
the three thousand a year went to Edward Walpole, the
next brother.[1] All these great patent offices were
sinecures; they were always executed by deputy; the
principal had not a week's work to do from the first
annual quarter-day to the last. We can imagine how
these rank abominations would stink in the nostrils of
the House of Commons and the Treasury to-day. Yet
it is worth remembering that Burke, when he proposed
his famous plan of economical reform (1780), though he
admitted that the magnitude of the profits in the great
patent offices called for reformation, still looked with
complacency on an Exchequer list filled with the
descendants of the Walpoles, the Pelhams, and the
Townshends, and maintained the expediency of these
indirect provisions for the families of great public
servants. Indirect rewards have long disappeared, and
nothing is more certain than that the whole system of
political pension, even as a direct and personal reward,
is drawing to an end. Whether either the purity or
the efficiency of political service will gain by the
change, is not so certain. Walpole at least can hardly
be censured for doing what, in the very height of

[1] See in Horace Walpole's *Letters*, the *Memorandum respecting
his Income*, p. lxxix, and i. 314. Also Coxe, ch. 61, iv. 320.

his zeal for reform, Burke seriously and deliberately
defended.

Abuse of patronage, however, was the least formidable
of the charges that descended year after year in a storm
on Walpole's head.   He was roundly and constantly
charged with sustaining a lavish private expenditure by
peculation from public funds.[1]   The palace which he
built for himself in Norfolk was matter for endless
scandal.   He planted gardens, people said, in places to
which the very earth had to be transported in waggons.
He set fountains flowing and cascades tumbling, where
water was to be conveyed by long aqueducts and costly
machines.   He was a modern Sardanapalus, imitating
the extravagance of Oriental monarchs at the expense of
a free people whom he was at once impoverishing and
betraying.   They described him as going down to his
country seat loaded with the spoils of an unfortunate
nation.   He had purchased most of the county of Norfolk, and held at least one-half of the stock of the Bank
of England.   It was plainly hinted that in view of a
possible impeachment at some future day, he had made
himself safe by investing one hundred and fifty thousand
pounds in jewels and plate as an easily portable form of

---

[1] Thus, in the popular doggerel of the day—

" But a few years ago,
As we very well know,
He scarce had a guinea his fob in ;
But by bribing of friends,
To serve his dark ends,
Now worth a full million is Robin.

" As oft hath he said
That our debts should be paid,
And the nation be eased of her throbbing ;
Yet on tick we still run,
For the true sinking fund
Is the bottomless pocket of Robin."

wealth. He had also secretly dispatched four hundred thousand pounds in a single year to bankers at Amsterdam, Vienna, and Genoa, to be ready for him in case of untoward accidents.

These lively fabrications undoubtedly represented the common rumour and opinion of the time, and were excellently fitted to nourish the popular dislike with which Walpole came to be regarded. They had their origin in the same suspicious temper towards an unpopular minister, which two generations before had made the people of London give to Clarendon's new palace in Piccadilly the name of Dunkirk House, and which a generation later prompted the charge that Lord Bute's great house and park at Luton had come out of the bribes of France. They had hardly more solid foundation than the charge of saturating Parliament with corruption. The truth seems to be that Walpole, like both the Pitts, was inexact and careless about money. Profusion was a natural element in a large, loose, jovial character like his, too incessantly preoccupied with business, power, government, and high affairs of State to have much regard for a wise private economy. He was supposed to contribute handsomely towards the expense of fighting elections.[1] He expended in building, adding, and improving at Houghton the sum of two hundred

---

[1] Coxe (ch. 45) quotes from Etough the utterly incredible story that Walpole spent 60,000*l.* out of his private fortune at the general election of 1734. Etough himself, I find, only says that he heard it after Walpole's death from somebody who had good information. The minister may have been profuse, but an expenditure of this magnitude would have been not profusion but insanity ; nor is it at all likely that he was at that time in a position to lay his hands upon so large an amount on his private credit.

thousand pounds. He built a lodge in Richmond Park at a cost of fourteen thousand pounds. His famous hunting congresses are said to have come to three thousand pounds a year—rather a moderate sum, according to the standard of to-day, for keeping open house for a whole county for several weeks in a vast establishment like Houghton. His collection of pictures was set down by Horace Walpole as having cost him forty thousand pounds more; but this I suspect to be a very doubtful figure, for according to a contemporary letter in Nichols's *Literary Anecdotes*, so many of the pictures were presents, that the whole cost could hardly have reached thirty thousand pounds; and it is worth noting that the famous Guido, the gem of the collection, while it cost him some six hundred pounds, was valued in the catalogue when it came to be sold to the Czarina at three thousand five hundred. For all this outlay, his foes contended that the income of his estate and the known salary of his offices were inadequate. They assumed, therefore, that the requisite funds were acquired by the sale of honours, places, and pensions, and by the plunder of the secret service money.

This charitable hypothesis is not really required by the facts, for we have a very tolerable explanation without it. In the first place, rents all over England had gone up by more than one-third, and in some counties they had much more than doubled themselves, since Walpole had come into his property. As I have stated, when his father died, in 1700, the rental of the Norfolk estates was upwards of two thousand pounds. Within forty years it is computed that it must have risen to

five thousand pounds.[1]   Secondly, his wife brought him
a fortune, which cleared the property of its embarrassments, and presumably left a margin.   Thirdly, his
firm and wise conviction of the folly of the South Sea
Scheme did not prevent him from turning his wisdom to account by dealing in South Sea stock.   "I
have just sold out," he said at one moment, "at a
thousand per cent, and I am fully satisfied."[2]   Even a
moderate transaction closed at a profit of a thousand
per cent would produce a substantial contribution
towards the building of Houghton or the purchase of
thirty thousand pounds worth of pictures.   Walpole's
success, it should be stated, was not due to any favour
from the South Sea promoters, such as ruined Aislabie,
Craggs, and Sunderland.   They hated him for his unvary-
ing denunciation of their project, and whatever money
he made in this way was due to his own penetration
and the good information which he got from his own
agents.   Fourth, when Walpole died, in 1745, he left a
heavy mortgage on Houghton, and a further debt of
fifty thousand pounds.   Fifth, he enjoyed the emoluments of his offices for five and twenty years.   This
item deserves some examination.

The amount of ministerial salaries in the eighteenth
century is only to be ascertained by search in the obscure
region of the issue books of the Exchequer, reports of

[1] This is Coxe's estimate, but in Mr. Ewald's *Life of Walpole*
(published in 1878) it is stated on the authority of a lately deceased
member of the Walpole family that the rental was under-stated by
Coxe (Ewald, p. 212).   Horace Walpole puts it at a nominal eight
thousand pounds a year.

[2] There is a not very intelligible passage in Lady Cowper's
Diary (p. 144) about Walpole's speculations.

select committees on finance and committees of inquiry, and various parliamentary returns of the civil and military establishments.[1] One remark may be made to begin with. During the reign of Queen Anne, and presumably down to a much later date, the modern punctuality of public payments was unknown. A Secretary of State makes light of having to write to a minister abroad apologising for her Majesty's backwardness in paying her servants. A minister at home, he says, can find some resources and make some shift or other to go on, but that those who serve abroad should be in arrears is indeed a great shame.[2] Even the most disinterested of public servants to-day may be startled to find a Secretary of State declaring that he had actually heard nothing of his regular salary for two years.[3] We may safely assume that a Chancellor of the Exchequer at least was able to protect himself against these inconvenient arrears in his own case.

Let us now see how much Walpole drew from the king's purse. From Godolphin's day down to the second administration of the Duke of Portland in 1807 there were invariably five lords of the Treasury when the Treasury was in commission. The allowance was 8000*l.* a year, which was divided into equal sums of 1600*l.* for each lord, reduced by various deductions to a net salary of 1220*l.* apiece. But the First Lord, in view of his great responsibilities, received additional pay out of the secret

---

[1] This task has been recently performed by Mr. Edward Hamilton, of the Treasury, a singularly competent hand, and I count myself fortunate in being able to give to my readers the benefit of some of the fruits of his diligent and exact inquiries.

[2] Bolingbroke's Letters, March 4, 1712-13.

[3] *Ibid.*, August 7, 1713.

service money, and this addition brought his net emoluments up to 5000*l.* a year. The payment of the First Lord continued to be made from the secret service money down to 1782, when the king by privy seal made better provision for him by an order that the whole of the salary allowed to the First Lord should henceforth be received at the Exchequer. This transfer of salary from secret service to the Civil List in 1782 was followed, as everybody knows, at the great resettlement of 1831 by its removal to the annual votes submitted to Parliament. We may take it as reasonably certain that Walpole received as First Lord the same sum from the secret service money, as is to-day voted to the same minister by the House of Commons. He also received a share of New Years' gifts, but the amount was trifling. There is no positive evidence that either the First Lord or the other Commissioners of the Treasury received anything out of the fee fund, though it may possibly have been a practice in those slovenly times for a First Lord to enrich himself out of perquisites. This, however, was not all. During the hundred years preceding Lord Liverpool's administration in 1812, the First Lord of the Treasury more often than not was also Chancellor of the Exchequer. Originally the salary of this office, combined as it was with that of Under Treasurer, was no more than the modest sum of 200*l.* A further addition of 1600*l.* was made in 1713 "in lieu of perquisites." After being discontinued for three years, this payment was revived in 1716 in favour of Sir Robert Walpole, and it afterwards formed a regular annual charge, bringing the emoluments of the Chancellor of the Exchequer, as such, up to 1800*l.* a year. He also received certain fees of

an average value of some 700*l.* a year.   The total annual
salary of the Chancellor of the Exchequer was therefore
in Walpole's time about 2400*l.*, and when, as in Walpole's
case, this office was held in conjunction with the post of
First Lord, the total income was about 7400*l.* a year.
Walpole, it may be observed, did not enjoy the salary
which came to Lord North, Mr. Pitt, and Lord Liverpool as Wardens of the Cinque Ports, and which, having
previously to 1778 been from 1100*l.* to 1500*l.* a year,
stood between that date and 1827, when it was abolished, at a substantial net figure not much below 3000*l*
While then two of his successors at the head of the
Government before the end of the century drew 10,000*l.*
a year, Walpole's official income was almost exactly the
same as that which was attached to the two offices of
First Lord of the Treasury and Chancellor of the
Exchequer, when they were held together by the same
minister in 1873, and again from 1880 to 1882.[1]   To
this sum we must add some 2000*l.* a year for the patent
place in the Customs, making a gross total of over
9000*l.* a year of public money.   Let it be remarked, in
conclusion, that the king kept a very tight hand upon
the expenditure on secret service, and that the supposi-
tion that the minister was free to dip his hand into that
fund at his own discretion and pleasure, is a mere mis-
apprehension.

There is nothing unreasonable in supposing that Walpole's official income far exceeded any outlay in which it

[1] The two offices were not combined between 1817 and 1831,
except for a few months, when Mr. Canning was both First Lord
and Chancellor of the Exchequer.   Mr. Perceval is stated not to
have drawn the latter salary in 1810-11, when he held both
offices.

involved him. For those who exercise themselves in such matters, it is one of the great unsolved mysteries in human annals, how it came to pass that Mr. Pitt, who was unmarried, kept no great establishment, gave no sumptuous or costly entertainments, and who drew not much less than two hundred thousand pounds of public money, should yet have died fifty-two thousand pounds in debt. Whatever Pitt's secret may have been, Walpole's circumstances were tolerably clear. His sons were provided for at the public cost; he had a fortune with his wife; he made something of a fortune by speculation; his hospitality was ample, but there was no outrageous or unmeasured profusion; he had for twenty years an income from his lands and his offices of thirteen or fourteen thousand a year; and besides debt secured on mortgage, he owed fifty thousand pounds when he died. The account shows that like so many other great public benefactors, Walpole was no thrifty steward of his private fortunes, but it shows also that his expenditure can be perfectly explained out of known and avowed resources; that the imputation of personal corruption and private plunder—never openly made, be it observed, by any responsible person—is wholly unnecessary, gratuitous, and unsupported; and that the time has come when the reckless calumnies of unscrupulous opponents, striking with masks on, should be at last dropped finally out from the history of a good servant of his country.

CHAPTER VII

THE CABINET

THE great constitutional question of the eighteenth century, as every reader knows, was whether the government of the realm should be parliamentary or monarchical. Was it to be an absolute rule of the king; or, as Cromwell sought, a Parliament making laws and voting money, co-ordinate with the authority of the Chief Person, and not meddling with the executive; or a Parliament containing, nominating, guiding, and controlling its own executive? Walpole found it easiest, safest, and most natural to work steadily towards the last of these three systems. A secondary, but hardly less important question turned on the mechanism by which the system could best be made to work.

Walpole's vehement and effectual resistance to the Peerage Bill proved the strength of his conviction that a close aristocracy was not the system, nor the House of Lords the instrument, for smoothly and successfully conducting the national affairs. The lower House, besides its decisive prerogative of taxation, had the merit, in spite of venal potwallopers and territorial nominees, of containing a considerable representation of the new classes and new interests that were slowly asserting their

importance. The large towns, like Bristol and Newcastle, and the freeholders of counties, contributed a
strong independent element. Even the immense number
of nominees of the great families were probably not out
of proportion to their natural weight and influence. In
dealing with the House of Commons a minister was
dealing with the living and social forces of the country
in all their variety. The first question was how to
organise them for practical purposes, and Walpole
answered it by the principle of Party. He founded his
government directly on the support of a Whig majority
in the House of Commons, though that majority was in
great part due to the assent of powerful members of the
House of Lords. The second question was how to keep
administration in gear with the party majority, and
Walpole's solution was a party Cabinet. The Cabinet
system was the key to parliamentary monarchy.

The Act of Settlement did much more than regulate
the succession. The Tories consoled themselves by
inserting two restrictive constitutional provisions of
very remarkable scope. One was an attempt to revive
the authority of the Privy Council, by ordaining that all
such matters and things pertaining to the government
of the realm as are by law and custom properly cog-
nisable in the Privy Council, should be transacted there,
and that all resolutions taken there should be signed by
such Privy Councillors as should advise and consent to
the same. This clause was levelled at the practice which
had grown up under Charles II and his brother, of governing through a select Cabinet of the king's servants, to the
detriment, as was supposed, both of the Privy Council as a
whole, and of the lawful power and authority of Parliament.

Another provision of the Act of Settlement shows in a still stronger light how little shaped were the constitutional ideas of the day, and has special bearings on Walpole's share in our constitutional development. It enacted that no holder of office under the king should be capable of serving as a member of the House of Commons. A section of only a couple of lines was thus enough, by excluding ministers from the representative House, to divorce the executive from the legislative branch of government. This was by no means in the mind or intention of the framers of the Bill. What they desired was to put a stop to the corruption of members of Parliament by places and pensions from the Crown. The section would have been a remedy for the evil at which it was aimed, but it would have fundamentally transformed the constitution of this country as we understand it, and at the same time all those numerous constitutions which are derived or imitated from our own.

Both clauses were repealed in the early part of the reign of Anne; they never, therefore, came into operation, but they have an interest of their own in this place. Walpole's work in shaping the constitution may be described as fixing it on the very foundations which the fourth and sixth sections of the Act of Settlement would have made impossible. In other words, the effect of his policy, when it was finally carried through, was to establish the Cabinet on a definite footing as the seat and centre of the executive government, to maintain the executive in the closest relation with the legislature, to govern through the legislature, and to transfer the power and authority of the Crown to the House of Commons. Some writers have held that the first Ministry in the

modern sense was that combination of Whigs whom
William called to aid him in government in 1695.
Others contend that the second administration of Lord
Rockingham, which came into power in 1782, after the
triumph of the American colonists, the fall of Lord
North, and the defeat of George III, was the earliest
ministry of the type of to-day. At whatever date we
choose first to see all the decisive marks of that remarkable system which combines unity, steadfastness, and
initiative in the executive, with the possession of supreme
authority alike over men and measures by the House of
Commons, it is certain that it was under Walpole that
its ruling principles were first fixed in parliamentary
government, and that the Cabinet system received the
impression that it bears in our own time.

This is not the place for any inquiry into the black-
letter learning relating to the various royal or national
councils. The name of Cabinet Council, according to
the books, first occurs casually in Bacon's *Essays*. Sir
Walter Raleigh gave the name of Cabinet Council to his
curious collection of political and polemical aphorisms.
As a piece of mechanism, a Cabinet is first heard of in
the reign of Charles I., and is mentioned both by
Clarendon and Pepys. Charles II made certain well-
known experiments in the same direction, but no
monarch with Charles's absolutist leanings could desire
to set up any body of private advisers in an established
position, within either the letter of the law or the spirit
of the constitution. The growth of the Cabinet system
has been as gradual, and as apparently fortuitous, as
most other articles of our constitutional development.
Neither the theory, nor the actual rules and marks of

this peculiar institution, have been put into shape even by this time; much less was any theory of it present to the minds of statesmen in the eighteenth century. The practice was not uniform, and depended on the cohesion of parties, on the exigencies of the moment, and on the temper or the position of the sovereign and of the minister.

It is really in the reign of Queen Anne that the system comes into pretty clear outline. Godolphin forced Sunderland upon the queen in 1706, and he compelled her to remove Harley afterwards. Each of these steps was prompted by the victory of the Whigs in the elections of 1705. So far as it went, this was a recognition of two main principles of the modern system: first, that the chief adviser of the Crown chooses his colleagues; and next, that a Cabinet depends upon a majority in the House of Commons. But neither principle made very rapid way.

How unsettled were the notions attached to the term of Cabinet, is curiously illustrated in a parliamentary incident of 1711. A motion had been put down, of censure on the Cabinet Council for causing misfortunes in Spain. When the motion came on, the wording was found to have been altered, so as to direct it, not against the Cabinet, but against ministers. The alteration gave rise to a singular discussion. The mover justified it on the ground that the word ministers was better known than the words Cabinet Council. Lord Cowper thought one term just as objectionable as the other: Cabinet was unknown in our law; both were vague; the House ought to know what minister was aimed at, and whether more than one was intended. A third speaker held that there was no distinction between Ministry and Cabinet. A fourth replied, truly enough

from the modern point of view, that Ministry is more
extensive than Cabinet. Peterborough interposed with
a witty remark that the Privy Council were such as
were thought to know everything and knew nothing,
while the Cabinet Council were those who thought that
nobody knew anything but themselves.[1]

No fewer than three distinct bodies are to be recognised during the reign of Anne as taking part in the
transaction of public business, apart from the deliberations of Parliament on the one hand, and the executive
orders of the Secretary of State on the other. First,
the treaties of peace and commerce in 1713 are described
as having been read in the Great Council, and there
ordered to be ratified.[2] This was evidently little more
than a merely formal proceeding, without debate, like
those of the Privy Council in modern days. It seems
that some criticism was offered, but it was resented by
Bolingbroke as unusual and meaningless. After the
suspicion that had prompted the clause in the Act of
Settlement, ministers would hardly have felt themselves
safe in ratifying so momentous a set of instruments as
the Treaties of Utrecht without this solemnity. A writer
of the time, for instance, quoted by Hallam, lays it down
that the chancellor could only make himself safe in
setting the great seal to foreign alliances, on condition
that a matter of that consequence had been first debated
and resolved in council.[3] The whole circumstances of
the Peace of Utrecht were so full of peril to the
ministers concerned, as later events showed, that the

[1] *Parl. Hist.*, vi. 971.

[2] *Bolingbroke's Letters*, 29th September 1713.

[3] See in Lord Campbell's life of Lord King, *Lives of Chancellors*,
c. 125.

desire to make himself as safe as he could was something very different from the scruple of a constitutional pedant, and simply sprang from natural anxiety to keep his head on his shoulders.   There is no reason to suppose that Walpole and the Marlborough Whigs were invited to the Great Council on this occasion, any more than the Opposition is invited on similar occasions now.

Second, mention is frequently made of a body of which all trace has now disappeared.   It is called sometimes Committee of Council, and sometimes Lords of the Council, and it met usually at the Cockpit in Whitehall.   This body was evidently more restricted than the Privy Council; it was less restricted than the Cabinet Council, and it was different from the Cabinet in composition.[1]   It was perhaps composed with a particular view to collecting the opinion of specialists.   Its proceedings were not purely formal ; it really discussed and transacted business, just as the Cabinet discusses and transacts it now, and as no other executive body does now excepting the Cabinet.   The preliminary negotiations of the Treaty of Utrecht were first disclosed to the Lords at the Cockpit, and repeatedly debated and authorised by them.   Foreign envoys argued their case before them. They authorised the instructions to Lord Strafford on his important mission to the Hague in 1711.   They

---

[1] In a letter of Bolingbroke's (15th December 1711) he talks of "the Committee of Council not sitting till to-morrow night, nor the Cabinet till Monday." They were evidently therefore two distinct bodies. Other passages in Bolingbroke's letters referring to this Committee of Council are as follows : 2d October and 26th October 1711 ; 4th September, 13th September, 12th November 1713 ; 11th February 1713-14.

were brought into action in settling the instructions to Mr. Harley when he was dispatched to Hanover two years later. We can only conjecture that the Lords of the Committee of Council were selected by the Secretary of State, with the express approval, possibly even on the personal initiative, of the queen; and were brought together upon occasions of moment, when it was desired to clothe great executive acts with peculiar authority and solemnity. The Privy Council always worked through committees. The Lords at the Cockpit were probably a committee especially formed for foreign affairs, just as the committee where Harley was stabbed by Guiscard was a judicial committee, taking cognisance of a charge of high treason. Walpole appointed a committee of the Privy Council to report to Parliament on the charges of corruption against Lord Macclesfield. Against this view, however, that the Lords at Whitehall were a committee on foreign affairs, analogous to the later committee for trade and plantations, we have to set the circumstance that it was at a meeting of this Committee of Council, assembled first at the Cockpit, and thence suddenly called to Kensington by the alarming condition of the queen, that the famous scene took place which I have already described (p. 38).[1] So far as I know, there is no later reference to it. Whatever may have been the functions of this committee, it was evidently a ministerial council, and the intrusion of the opposition Lords was an irregularity. The committee may be regarded as a compromise between the old and

[1] The failure to distinguish this body from the Council at large explains the obscurity and confusion of ordinary accounts of what happened on that memorable day.

venerated institution of the Privy Council, and the new, the immature, and the jealously suspected institution of the Cabinet. It is not improbable that privy councillors who were not in office sometimes attended this intermediate committee. If so, it was a sort of example for those conferences which took place in the Parliament of 1868 between the Prime Minister and Lord Cairns in reference to the details of the two great Irish measures of the Government, and again in 1884, between the Prime Minister of the day and the leader of the Opposition, to settle the redistribution of parliamentary seats. There are those who believe circumstances to be without difficulty conceivable under which a select body of eminent privy councillors might come together to take part in deliberation, and thus might make the chief men of both parties jointly responsible for some great act of State. Speculations of this kind, however, must be viewed with lively suspicion by everybody who believes that party is an essential element in the wholesome working of parliamentary government. Such joint responsibility would destroy party; and its growth in practice might easily be used both to revive the decaying power of the House of Lords, and even to restore disused authority to any sovereign who might try to press every question in which he happened to feel an interest, towards this method of joint solution.

The third group of advisers was the Cabinet. Down to the end of Walpole's time they are referred to as Lords of the Cabinet or Lords of the Cabinet Council. The Cabinet is now an informal committee of the Privy Council, which in time superseded in effect all other groups formed within that body, and became, as everybody

knows, clothed with attributes of its own of the highest
novelty and importance. Certain offices, such as that of
First Commissioner of the Admiralty,[1] always brought
their holder into Cabinet. So did the Lord-Lieutenancy
of Ireland.[2] Some great personages always sat in the
Cabinet during the first half of the eighteenth century,
who sit there no longer. Lord Chancellor Hardwicke
describes a Cabinet Council in 1737, at which the
Archbishop of Canterbury was present, as well as the
Lord Chamberlain, the Master of the Horse, and the
Groom of the Stole. What is still more curious,
Bolingbroke, writing to tell the Bishop of Bristol, then
Lord Privy Seal and a plenipotentiary at Utrecht, that
the queen desires to make him Bishop of London,
consoles him for the change by the assurance that as the
head of the diocese of London he will keep his seat in
the Cabinet.[3] We are no more likely again to see a
prelate of the Church in the Cabinet, than we are again
to see one made Lord Keeper. When the inclusion of
the primate and the four great officers of the royal
household ceased, it is not easy to tell. In the first
Rockingham administration of 1765, the Cabinet contained the Duke of Portland as Lord Chamberlain, and
the Duke of Rutland as Master of the Horse. In Pitt's
administration which succeeded, the household officers do
not appear as of Cabinet rank ; and it may be that the
Great Commoner abolished that arrangement. It
certainly lasted down to the fall of Walpole.[4]

[1] Bolingbroke to Strafford, 12th August 1712.
[2] Stanhope to Walpole, 16th January 1717.
[3] 2d September 1763.
[4] See Hervey's.*Memoirs*, iii. 353 ; Harris's *Life of Hardwicke*, i.
365, 404, etc.

Some curious expressions linger very late. For instance, after the Pelhams had routed Granville and Lord Bath in 1746, and when the latter held no office, they made it one of their conditions with the king that Bath "might be out of the Cabinet Council." [1] There could be no question now of the victors in a contest for power bargaining that their defeated rivals should be excluded from attendance at Cabinets as well as from office. Again, it has often been remarked that in the younger Pitt's first Cabinet he was the only commoner; but throughout the eighteenth century Cabinets were mainly composed of peers. It was remarked as an extraordinary proof of Walpole's power that in 1733 he insisted on giving the post of First Lord of the Admiralty to Sir Charles Wager, though no commoner had been thought worthy of that office since the accession of the House of Brunswick. The king made Wager's want of family distinction an express ground of objection, and what is more curious, the veteran himself thought a purely imaginary genealogy a better recommendation than his real services. In Hervey's list of the Cabinet at the close of Walpole's Government, Wager and Sir Robert are the only two commoners. In the Pelham Government, which after a very short interval succeeded Walpole, Henry Pelham was the only commoner in the Cabinet, and Pelham, like the younger Pitt, was himself the son and the brother of a peer.[2]

A very remarkable incident occurred a few years after

[1] Coxe's *Pelham*, i. 295.

[2] Of this Cabinet we have that rare record, an account of a division, with a list of those who voted aye and no respectively. See the Introduction to Mr. Yorke's *Parliamentary Journal*.

Walpole's death.   A certain person asserted that he had
heard a bishop, the Solicitor-General, and another, drink at
table to the health of the Pretender.   He was summoned
before the Cabinet Council, put on his oath, and interro-
gated ; and after hearing the other side, the Cabinet
reported to the king.   On this proceeding a debate was
raised in the House of Lords, in which strong language
was used against what had been done, as a revival of
the Star Chamber, the Holy Inquisition, and so forth : it
was no Committee of Council ; it had no more legal
authority than any private meeting of lords ; it was an
attempt to erect a new jurisdiction.   The Lord Chancellor cited an earlier instance of this very extraordinary
proceeding, but there seems to be no later.[1]

The same reluctance existed in the first forty years
of the century, that has been so constantly felt by wise
ministers since, to make precedents for enlarging the
Cabinet.   The queen had much rather confine than
extend it, says Bolingbroke.   Unfortunately circumstances have set so strongly in the contrary direction
during recent years, and the number of ministers almost
necessarily included in a Cabinet has grown so large,
that it seems as if the result must inevitably be the
formation of an interior junto, small enough to allow of
deliberation and decision at close quarters.   This will
be no more than a return to the system of Walpole's
time—a large Cabinet, but the effective body composed
of himself, the Chancellor, and the two Secretaries of
State.   Walpole, as we might have expected from his
character, called meetings of the Cabinet as seldom as

[1] For a full account see Coxe's *Pelham Administration*, ch. xxx.
ii. 254-263.

possible. His habit was to invite two or three of his colleagues specially acquainted with the business in hand to dine with him, and then he settled it. The regular Cabinet dinner was an informal device of a later age, marked by the peculiarity and possible convenience that no minute of the topics of discussion was necessarily sent to the sovereign, as in the case of formal meetings of the Cabinet. The Cabinet dinner seems to have been dropped as a practice for the last thirty years. It was in full vogue during the Aberdeen Government, but fell into abeyance under Lord Palmerston, who always cared mainly for national defence and foreign relations, and did not choose to sacrifice a social evening to talk about miscellaneous business.

Perhaps the most important of all the distinctions between the Cabinet in its rudimentary stage at the beginning of the century and its later practice, remains to be noticed. Queen Anne held a Cabinet every Sunday, at which she was herself present, just as we have seen that she was present at debates in the House of Lords. With a doubtful exception in the time of George III, no sovereign has been present at a meeting of the Cabinet since Anne, though George II presided on one memorable occasion at a meeting of the Privy Council, which is not easily to be distinguished from a Cabinet.[1] This vital change was probably due to the accident that Anne's successor did not understand the language in which its deliberations were carried on.

[1] Lord Waldegrave in his *Memoirs* mentions a meeting of "the king's principal servants," to consider the Prince of Wales's establishment in 1756. Some of the books take his language to mean that the king was present, but the implication is clearly the other way.

The withdrawal of the sovereign from Cabinet Councils was essential to the momentous change which has transferred the whole substance of authority and power from the Crown, to a committee chosen by one member of the two Houses of Parliament, from among other members.

There are other illustrations of the change that has taken place in this direction. For instance Queen Anne herself wrote dispatches to her generals and ministers abroad. Again, when Buys, the Dutch Pensionary, came over to argue against the Peace, he had a private audience of the queen, the Secretary of State no doubt being present. The envoy made her a long discourse. She listened to him with great patience, told him that the burdens of the war were too heavy to be longer borne, and desired him to confer with her ministers, meaning, however, the Committee of Council, and not ministers in Cabinet.[1] Maffei had a similar interview on the part of Savoy. No foreign envoy would now be allowed to address the sovereign personally upon national business, though the distinctive mark of an ambassador is that he is, and a minister is not, entitled to personal access to the sovereign. In modern practice, when the Secretary of State introduces an ambassador, it is the Secretary who breaks the seal of the letter of credit before the ambassador presents it to the queen.

Passing from the sovereign to her ministers, we find the relations of the Secretary of State to the Cabinet, at least during the negotiations of the Peace of Utrecht, such as would now be held distinctly unconstitutional. St. John, when Secretary of State, invites the British

[1] Bolingbroke's Correspondence, 23d October 1711.

representatives abroad to keep up a double correspondence with him, and to write not merely "letters containing
the general thread of business which are read in Cabinet,"
but also private letters with such secret particulars
as may not be properly communicated even to the
Cabinet till the queen should think fit. He explains as
one of the advantages of these personal letters that the
minister is under no obligation to leave them behind
him in his office.[1] No doubt, private and unofficial
correspondence of that kind is still a common channel
of important information, but no minister would
deliberately hide it from his colleagues for purposes of
his own, as Louis XV worked his sinister system of
double correspondence against his own servants. Bolingbroke goes much farther. He even sends to the ambassador the project of the Peace, without having
communicated it to the Cabinet.[2] The memorable decision to create twelve peers in a day was taken without
reference to the body, whose collective assent to so
momentous a step would to-day be regarded as not any
less indispensable a preliminary, than the assent of the
sovereign herself.[3]

It is easy to see to what point the evolution of
Cabinet government was brought in Walpole's time and
by his influence. Two circumstances were essential to
the growth of this form of government in the British
type. One was the absence of the sovereign, of which
I have already spoken. How great a difference that
makes, was shown by the effect of Louis XVIII and Louis

---

[1] To Lord Bath, 8th May 1711.
[2] 6th April and 6th May 1711.
[3] To Strafford, 1st January 1711.

Philippe sitting at the head of the table, as the President of the French Republic now does, while their
ministers discussed business. The second essential is the
presence of ministers in the legislature. The founders
of the American constitution, as all know, followed
Montesquieu's phrases, if not his design, about separat-
ing legislature from executive, by excluding ministers
from both Houses of Congress. This is fatal to any
reproduction of the English system. The American
Cabinet is vitally unlike our own on this account.
If Walpole had taken the line afterwards adopted at
Philadelphia, ministerial responsibility would have borne
a very different sense from that with which we are now
so familiar, as almost to regard it as of divine ordinance.
In no direction did Walpole give a more important turn
to our affairs. He imparted a decisive bias at a highly
critical moment ; though the struggle was a long one, it
is to Walpole more especially that we owe it that
government in England is carried on, not by royal or
imperial ministers, as in Prussia, nor by popular ministers, as in the United States, but by parliamentary
ministers. In this view the reader will perhaps not
regard it as an irrelevant digression, if we devote a page
or two to recalling what government by parliamentary
ministers is, and how it is worked.

The principal features of our system of Cabinet
government to-day are four. The first is the doctrine
of collective responsibility. Each Cabinet minister
carries on the work of a particular department, and for
that department he is individually answerable. When
Pitt's administration came to an end in 1801, and Lord
Loughborough was displaced from the woolsack, the ex-

Chancellor, to the amazement of the new Prime Minister, kept the key of the Cabinet boxes, and actually, without being summoned, attended meetings of the Cabinet. At last Addington wrote to beg him to discontinue his attendance, on the principle that "the number of the Cabinet should not exceed that of the persons whose responsible situations in office require their being members of it." In addition to this individual responsibility, he shares to a very large extent a collective responsibility with all other members of the government, for anything of high importance that is done in every other branch of the public business besides his own. The question whether the mistakes or misdeeds of one minister involves all the rest, is of course not quite independent of the position of the minister, or of the particular action. The censure and impeachment of Lord Melville, for example, was so purely personal in its bearings that it did not break up the government of Mr. Pitt. But as a general rule every important piece of departmental policy is taken to commit the entire Cabinet, and its members stand or fall together. The Chancellor of the Exchequer may be driven from office by a bad dispatch from the Foreign office, and an excellent Home Secretary may suffer for the blunders of a stupid Minister of War. The Cabinet is a unit—a unit as regards the sovereign, and a unit as regards the legislature. Its views are laid before the sovereign and before Parliament, as if they were the views of one man. It gives its advice as a single whole, both in the royal closet, and in the hereditary or the representative chamber. If that advice be not taken, provided the matter of it appear to be of proper importance, then the Cabinet, before or after an appeal to the electors, dissolves itself and disappears. The first mark of the Cabinet, as that institution is now understood, is united and indivisible responsibility.

The second mark is that the Cabinet is answerable immediately to the majority of the House of Commons, and ultimately to the electors whose will creates that majority. Responsibility to the Crown is slowly ceasing to be more than a constitutional fiction, though even as a fiction it possesses many practical conveniences. William IV, it is true, dismissed the Melbourne Government in 1834 of his own motion, and Sir Robert Peel stuck to the helm for his hundred days in spite of a hostile majority. But though such experiments may by bare possibility recur, they will hardly recur often, and they will never last long. The only real responsibility is to the House of Commons. Responsibility to the House of Lords means no more than that that House may temporarily resist bills of which it disapproves, until the sense of the electors of the House of Commons has been taken upon them. Even in Walpole's time, when the House of Lords passed a motion of censure upon the Spanish Convention in 1739, the minister paid no attention to it.[1]

Third, the Cabinet is, except under uncommon, peculiar, and transitory circumstances, selected exclusively from one party. There have been coalitions of men of opposite parties, but in most cases, down to the present time, coalition has been only the preliminary of fusion. There have been conjunctions, again, of men openly holding directly opposite opinions on subjects

[1] Coxe, iv. 58.

going to the very foundations of government, and
turning on the very principles that mark party difference.   Lord Liverpool's Ministry, for instance, lasted for
fourteen years, with so important an issue as Catholic
emancipation left an open question.   But notwithstanding both coalitions and open questions, it remains
generally true that Cabinets are made from one
party.

Fourth, the Prime Minister is the keystone of the
Cabinet arch.   Although in Cabinet all its members
stand on an equal footing, speak with equal voice,
and, on the rare occasions when a division is taken, are
counted on the fraternal principle of one man, one vote,
yet the head of the Cabinet is *primus inter pares*, and
occupies a position which, so long as it lasts, is one of
exceptional and peculiar authority.   It is true that he is
in form chosen by the Crown, but in practice the choice
of the Crown is pretty strictly confined to the man who
is designated by the acclamation of a party majority.
If a party should chance to be divided or uncertain as
to its leader, then undoubtedly, the favour of the Crown
might suffice to turn the balance.   There might be some
exaggeration in saying that the veto of the Crown on a
First Minister is virtually as dead as its veto on a bill;
still the Crown could hardly exercise any real power
either of selection or exclusion against the marked
wishes of the constituencies.

The Prime Minister, once appointed, chooses his own
colleagues, and assigns to them their respective offices.
It sometimes happens that, in the case of very important
colleagues, they are almost as effectually designated to
him by public opinion and parliamentary position, as he is

himself designated to the sovereign for his own high office. Still, there is more than a margin for his free exercise of choice in the persons admitted to his Cabinet, and in all cases it is for him alone to settle the distribution of posts. Constitutional respect for the Crown would inspire a natural regard for the personal wishes of the sovereign in recommendations to office, but royal predilections or prejudices will undoubtedly be less and less able to stand against the Prime Minister's strong view of the requirements of the public service.

The flexibility of the Cabinet system allows the Prime Minister in an emergency to take upon himself a power not inferior to that of a dictator, provided always that the House of Commons will stand by him.   In ordinary circumstances he leaves the heads of departments to do their work in their own way.   It is their duty freely and voluntarily to call him into council, on business of a certain order of importance.   With the Foreign Secretary alone he is in close and continuous communication as to the business of his office.   Foreign affairs must always be the matter of continuous thought in the mind of the Prime Minister.   They are not continuously before the Cabinet ; it has not therefore the same fulness of information as the Prime Minister ; and consequently in this important department of public action, the Cabinet must for the most part, unless there be some special cause of excitement, depend upon the prudence and watchfulness of its head.

In case of differences arising between departments, it is to the Prime Minister that the appeal lies, and the regular course for a minister who is dissatisfied with his chief's decision is to retire.   Where the Prime Minister

is displeased with the language or the action of a colleague, he possesses, indeed, no direct prerogative to
call for his resignation, without going first to the sovereign and procuring her assent. But that assent could
practically never be refused to a Prime Minister with a
parliamentary majority, unless the sovereign were prepared to take new advisers and face a dissolution.
Though it is just conceivable that the sovereign might
remonstrate successfully against the minister's request
for a colleague's dismissal, yet it is not likely that a
minister would make a request of such moment without
intending to abide by it and to press it to the end.

An important qualification of the Prime Minister's
power exists in the case of the Crown. Here it is well
understood that the sovereign has a right to demand the
opinion of the Cabinet as a court of appeal against the
Prime Minister or any other minister. It is now publicly
known, for instance, that in the difficult foreign crisis of
1859-61 dispatches were frequently referred back by
the sovereign from the Foreign Secretary and the Prime
Minister to the Cabinet as a whole, and were there constantly modified in the sense desired. This is clearly
a practical power left to the Crown, and,if there chanced
to be a strong Cabinet, the use of such a power might
result in a considerable reduction of the Prime Minister's normal authority, and its transfer to the general
body of his colleagues.

In filling up the highest posts within a department,
such as the headship of the permanent staff, the nomina-
tion of an ambassador, or the appointment to governor-
ship of an important colony or the great dependency
of India, the Prime Minister, though not taking the

initiative, would still usually expect to be consulted by
the minister more directly concerned. Even the Lord
Chancellor is believed sometimes to go through the form of
consulting him in filling vacancies on the judicial bench.
Finally, just as the Cabinet has been described as being
the regulator of relations between Queen, Lords, and
Commons, so is the Prime Minister the regulator of
relations between the queen and her servants. "As
the Cabinet stands between the sovereign and Parliament, so the Prime Minister stands between the sovereign
and the Cabinet."[1] This does not mean that any minister is out of immediate communication with the Crown,
in matters strictly affecting his own department as to
which the Crown may desire to be informed; but only
that outside of these matters it is the Prime Minister
only who conveys to the sovereign the views of his colleagues. Such attempts to intrigue with the sovereign
against a colleague as were common with Sunderland,
Stanhope, Townshend, and Carteret, and as were long
afterwards repeated with particular baseness by Lord
Loughborough, when he secretly warned George III of
Pitt's Catholic policy and advised him against it, are,
we may be very confident, never likely to recur.

Here this too long digression may end. Hardly
one of these four principles was accepted by Walpole, or by anybody else in his time, with the accuracy
or the fulness with which they are all acted upon
at present. They all coloured and shaped the new
form that popular government was putting on, but
neither the joint solidarity of the Cabinet, nor its direct
responsibility as the servant of Parliament, had yet

---

[1] Mr. Gladstone's *Gleanings*, i. 236, etc.

approached maturity.   Walpole undoubtedly made a
long stride towards establishing the doctrine of Cabinet
solidarity.   When he pressed for the dismissal of the
Duke of Roxburgh in 1752, he did so on the ground that
"the present administration is the first that was ever yet
known to be responsible for the whole government,
with a Secretary of State for one part of the kingdom
who, they are assured, acts counter to all their measures."
Yet when Carteret made his famous motion for Walpole's
removal in 1741, Lord Wilmington, though he held the
office of Privy Seal, did not vote in Walpole's defence
against the motion.   The cardinal question of the position
of the Prime Minister was in a most singular stage, for
Walpole was in practice able to invest himself with more
of the functions and powers of a Prime Minister than any
of his successors, and yet was compelled by the feeling of
the time earnestly and profusely to repudiate both the name
and title, and every one of the pretensions that it involves.

The earliest instance in which I have found the head
of the government designated as the Premier is in a
letter to the Duke of Newcastle from the Duke of Cumberland in 1746, though in Johnson's *Dictionary*, published
nine years later, *premier* still only figures as an adjective.
The king wished Pitt, then just made Paymaster, to
move the parliamentary grant to the victor of Culloden.
"I should be much better pleased," writes the Duke of
Cumberland, "if the Premier moved it, both as a friend
and on account of his weight.   I am fully convinced of
the Premier's goodwill to me."[1]   On the other hand, in

---

[1] Coxe's *Pelham Administration*, i. 486.   The Duchess of Marlborough in her Correspondence frequently speaks of "the Premier
Minister," but never of the Premier,—vol. ii. 152, 181, etc.

a debate so late as 1761, George Grenville declared that Prime Minister is an odious title, and he was sorry that it was now deemed an essential part of the constitution. Lord North is said never to have allowed himself in his own family to be called Prime Minister.

A flood of light is shed upon the advance that was made in the conception of this organ in government, by comparing Walpole's professions before the middle of the century, with those of Mr. Pitt at the end of it. Pitt's view of the position of the Prime Minister was stated in the well-known letter of Lord Melville to Addington in 1803. Addington had absurdly suggested that Mr. Pitt should return to the government either as Secretary of State or Chancellor of the Exchequer. Lord Chatham was to be the head of the administration. As might have been expected, the man who had for nearly twenty years been at the head of affairs in times of unexampled emergency, laughed at the proposal. He said satirically that he really had not the curiosity to ask what office he was to fill. He desired Lord Melville, however, to explain his views to Addington. Mr. Pitt, wrote Lord Melville, "stated not less pointedly and decidedly his sentiments with regard to the absolute necessity there is in the conduct of the affairs of this country, that there should be an avowed and real minister, possessing the chief weight in the council, and the principal place in the confidence of the king. In that respect there can be no rivalry or division of power. That power must rest in the person generally called the First Minister, and that minister ought, he thinks, to be the person at the head of the finances. He knows, to his own comfortable experience, that notwithstanding the abstract truth of that general proposition, it is noways incompatible with the most cordial concert and mutual exchange of advice and inter-course amongst the different branches of executive departments ; but still, if it should come unfortunately to such a radical difference of opinion that no spirit of conciliation or concession can reconcile, the sentiments of the minister must be allowed and understood to prevail, leaving the other members of administration to act as they may conceive themselves conscientiously called upon to act under the circumstances." [1]

What Pitt here arrogates to the minister as his just claim and demand, Walpole was obliged to thrust away from himself as a reproach and an offence against the constitution of the realm. When the great attack was opened upon him in 1741, Carteret expressly described as one of his worst misdemeanours, that he had usurped the sole power of directing all public affairs, and recommending to all public posts, honours, and employments. It was repeated as an article of charge against him in every speech, that he solely enjoyed and engrossed the ear of his sovereign. They called him a second Strafford, who excluded every man that disdained to be his slave from the pay and even from the smiles of the court. Mr. Sandys, who led the attack in the Commons, declared that : "According to our constitution we can have no sole and prime minister; we ought always to have several prime ministers or officers of state ; every such officer has his own proper department ; and no officer ought to meddle in the affairs belonging to the department of another." In arrogantly despising this fundamental

[1] Stanhope's *Life of Pitt*, iv. 24.

principle, Walpole had been guilty of a most heinous crime against the constitution. The attack was repulsed in both Houses, but the minority in the Lords drew up a protest, and the opening clause in it runs thus : "We are persuaded that a sole, or even a First Minister, is an officer unknown to the law of Britain, inconsistent with the constitution of this country, and destructive of liberty in any government whatsoever."

In Walpole's defence, neither he, nor any of those who spoke for him, contradicted this principle; they only denied the allegations of fact. The Bishop of Salisbury could find no proof that Walpole had usurped the authority of First Minister. The Lord Chancellor put his apology for Walpole's interference in patronage no higher than that, as there happened to be a very good correspondence among his Majesty's ministers, applicants for places came to Walpole, not because he had the ear of the king, but as the shortest way to the ear of the minister who had the place to give away. Walpole himself paid little attention to this particular charge in his reply, but in deprecating it he took up a remarkable position, to which neither Mr. Pitt nor any of his successors would have assented. "I do not pretend," he said, "to be a great master of foreign affairs; in that post it is not my business to meddle; and as one of his Majesty's council, I have only one voice." Notwithstanding this disclaimer, Walpole was undoubtedly an example of the important political truth, of which Mr. Pitt and Sir Robert Peel are equally conspicuous illustrations, that no administrations are so successful as those where the distance in parliamentary authority, party influence, and popular position, between the Prime Minister and his colleagues in the Cabinet, is wide, recognised, and decisive.

In concluding this portion of my subject, it is proper to remark that it would be very misleading to take the arrangements of any one period, whether 1889 or 1740 or any other date, as being definitely fixed parts of the constitution.   To-day it is correct to say that the Cabinet has drawn to itself all, and more than all, of the royal power over legislation, as well as many of the most important legislative powers of Parliament.   With due qualifications and allowances, it is not very far from the mark to add that the head of the Cabinet to-day corresponds in many particulars, alike in the source of his power and in the scope of his official jurisdiction, with the President of the United States,—though with the two immensely important and far-reaching distinctions, that the minister holds office for no fixed term, and that he always sits in the legislature.   It is possible that within the next hundred years government by Cabinet may undergo changes of substance as important as the changes since the time of Sir Robert Walpole; but it is worthy of remark that the living statesman of widest experience and highest authority in the working of our constitutional system, has declared that in his judgment the Cabinet as a great organ of government has now found its final shape, attributes, functions, and permanent ordering.

CHAPTER VIII

WHEN historians blame Walpole for not attempting reforms, they lose sight of a leading chapter in his policy : they omit his vigorous and fruitful efforts in the field of trade and commerce, which was then of far greater national importance than any merely political or parliamentary changes. His biographer is in the right when he complains that men have thought too exclusively of the minister's triple alliances, quadruple alliances, and foreign treaties; have made too much of the charges of ambition and corruption brought against him by unbridled faction; and have left those salutary regulations which ought to render the name of Walpole dear to every Englishman, to be principally confined to books of rates and taxes.[1] Walpole opened this chapter in what was, for the time, a remarkable proposition. In 1721 the king's speech contained a paragraph foreshadowing reforms, compared with which bills for abolishing places or shortening parliaments were but as flies on the legislative wheel. "We should be extremely wanting to ourselves," the king was made to say, "if we neglected to improve the favourable opportunity given

[1] Coxe, ch. xxii.

us of extending our commerce, upon which the riches and grandeur of this nation chiefly depend. It is very obvious that nothing would more conduce to the obtaining so public a good, than *to make the exportation of our own manufactures, and the importation of the commodities used in the manufacturing of them, as practicable and as easy as may be.*" Harley and Bolingbroke had made an ineffectual opening in the direction of free trade, in the abortive treaty of commerce with France at the time of Utrecht;[1] and to that extent Lord Beaconsfield was justified in a favourite contention of his responsible days, that peace and free trade were the original property of Tory statesmen. But the royal speech of 1721 is the first full, general, and distinct approach, so far as I know, made by an English statesman towards those enlightened views of trade which were fifty-five years later given in systematic shape to the world by the genius of Adam Smith. Walpole was as good as his word; he persuaded Parliament in the session of 1721 to remove duties on export from one hundred and six articles of British manufacture, and duties on import from thirty-eight articles of raw material.

Nine years later (1730) he conferred a more indisputable boon on the trade with Georgia and Carolina. The narrow policy of those times restricted the colonies to an exclusive intercourse with the mother country. Walpole passed an Act allowing the Carolina and Georgian planters to export their rice direct to any port in Europe

---

[1] It has been pointed out that Arthur Moore, a commissioner of plantations, who was the real author of Bolingbroke's commercial treaty with France, had become, on Bolingbroke's return in 1725, a close ally of Walpole.—(Mr. Harrop's *Bolingbroke*, pp. 149 and 245.)

south of Finisterre, provided they sent it in British ships, manned by British sailors. The result was that the rice of the American plantations beat the rice of Egypt and northern Italy out of the markets of Europe. Shortly before his fall, he carried a measure for allowing the West Indian traders to export sugar direct to foreign countries, provided it were in British bottoms, without first landing it in British ports. The growth of colonial trade was one of the most striking facts of Walpole's time. A dozen years before he went to the Treasury the whole trade with the plantations—about 1,300,000*l.*, both export and import—was only a few thousand pounds more under the head of export, and it was a third less in import, than that which was carried on with Jamaica alone, five and twenty years after Walpole left the Treasury. In the same interval, the total export trade from England with all the world had risen from six million pounds a year to more than twelve millions.[1]

These were not mere hand-to-mouth expedients, but the outcome of enlightened and comprehensive views. Shortly after the failure of the excise scheme, which I shall have next to describe, a retired deputy-governor of Virginia came over to Walpole with a plan for an American tax. "No," said the minister, "I have old England set against me, and do you think I will have the new England likewise?" A few years later (1739) the temptation was renewed. Walpole again repelled it. His object had always been, he said, to encourage colonial commerce, because the greater the prosperity of the colonies, the greater would be their demand for English goods; and that was the true way in which to

---

[1] Burke's *Observations on Present State of the Nation.*

turn colonies into a source of wealth to a mother country. Walpole was content with seeing that no trouble came from America. He left it to the Duke of Newcastle, and the Duke left it so much to itself, that he had a closet full of despatches from American governors which had lain unopened for years. This was what Burke described as treating the colonies with salutary neglect, and what caused it to be said that George Grenville lost America because he was foolish enough to read the American despatches.

The most famous of all Walpole's projects in taxation, in the sense of being that which made most noise, was the scheme for extending the excise. This gave his enemies their first serious advantage over him, and inflicted on his power the first important check. In itself the new policy of excise offered no striking or imposing features. The most important element of it, the facility for warehousing imported goods for re-exportation free of duty, had been in operation for many years in Holland. Indeed, it was the minister's object to narrow his design within the smallest possible compass, and to present its novelty at the lowest. The bill actually introduced to the House of Commons (1733) was simply a proposal to turn the customs duty on the importation of tobacco into an excise duty on its consumption. Instead of paying duty, or giving bonds, on landing the tobacco from Maryland or Virginia on the quays of London or Bristol, the merchant was to lodge his hogsheads in warehouses under the control of excise officers; to pay duty only as he took it out for home consumption; and if he took it out, not for the home market, but for re-exportation abroad, then he became free of all payments to the revenue whatever. The same system was to be extended to wine. Various advantages were claimed for the change. First, it would put an end to sundry gross frauds upon the revenue, from smuggling on an immense scale, down to abuses, petty and great, which the ingenuity of dishonest merchants, practising on discounts, allowances, and drawbacks, and the more primitive rapacity of lightermen, watermen, and gangsmen, devised and boldly carried on at every port in the island. Second, the prevention of these frauds and the decrease of smuggling would be a gain to the honest trader. Third, accompanied as it was by a simplification of rates, this cheaper and easier collection would be such an advantage to the revenue as to enable the Chancellor of the Exchequer to please the country gentlemen by taking a shilling off the land tax. Fourth, and much the most important of all, it would tend to make London a free port, and by consequence the market of the world.

It would be ridiculous in the light of modern experience to waste a single line in vindicating the great policy to which Walpole's Tobacco Bill was the opening. The author of the *Wealth of Nations*,[1] writing more than forty years later, had still to lament that none of Walpole's successors had dared to resume a project which in his case factions, politicians, and smuggling merchants successfully resisted. Walpole knew beforehand something of what he had to expect. But though Walpole was cautious and circumspect, he was no craven. He knew that his case was thoroughly sound, and without having any transcendent opinion of human integrity, he had faith in the efficacy of plain reason addressed to

[1] Bk. v. ch. ii.

solid interests. The Sacheverell episode and the South
Sea episode might have taught him the liability of his
countrymen to epidemics of unreason, and he was now
to see one of these epidemics sweep over them with a
violence that shook his power to its foundations.

The bare rumour of his politic design was followed
by the fiercest popular outcry that Walpole or any other
minister in our history ever encountered. The Opposition espied their chance, and eagerly seized it. A loud
note of alarm was raised from one end of the kingdom
to the other. The writers of the *Craftsman* brought to
bear on a project which was not yet before them, and
which they neither understood nor intended to understand, all their powers of wit, misrepresentation, and
ingenious calumny. No assertion was too wild, no
insinuation too incredible, no lie too glaring. Popular
ignorance, prejudice, and passion, when once thoroughly
roused, are never critical, and any charge was good
enough to hurl at "that plan of arbitrary power, that
monster, the excise." The proposal to put an excise duty
on tobacco and wine became swollen into a general
excise. Food, clothing, and all the other necessaries of
life were to be loaded with a crushing tax. Every man's
house would be invaded at every hour by the excise
officer. Every man's goods and all his dealings would
be exposed to minute and ceaseless inquisition. A great
standing army of revenue officers would be created, who
would overturn Magna Charta, undermine Parliament,
and degrade Englishmen as low as the wretched slaves
on the other side of the British Channel. The whole
country resounded with shouts of " *No slavery, no excise,
no wooden shoes.*" Are we to sacrifice the constitution,

cried Wyndham, only to prevent a few frauds on the revenue ? I had rather beg my bread from door to door, said Sir John Barnard, and see my country flourish, than be the greatest subject in the nation and see the trade of my country decaying, and the people enslaved and oppressed. Pulteney, with more wit but no less extravagance, said the minister's fine undertaking put him in mind of Sir Epicure Mammon in the *Alchemist*, who was promised the philosopher's stone, by which he was to get mountains of gold and everything that he could desire, but all ended at last in some little thing for curing the itch.

There were few boroughs that did not dispatch positive directions to their members to resist any new excise. The citizens of London, who might have been expected to resist the frenzy, were in as great a ferment as people in obscurer places. They sent a petition with the extraordinary prayer that they might be heard by counsel against the new tax, and it was brought by ten citizens in a train of coaches that reached all the way from Westminster to Temple Bar. The beadle and the summoning officer went round every parish in the city, beating up a mob to waylay members at the doors of Parliament. Even the soldiers took it into their heads that the excise would raise the price of their tobacco, and were declared by their generals to be as ripe for mutiny as the nation for rebellion.

The House of Commons kept itself pretty steady. After Walpole had explained and defended his plan, he held his men so well together, considering the vehemence of the cry out of doors, that when the division was taken on the first resolution it was carried by 266

against 205.   As the clamour grew more tremendous,
the numbers went down at each of the successive stages
of the measure, until at length the majority of sixty-one
on the main question had on a subsidiary issue sunk to
seventeen.   From the opening of the session until the
middle of April, Walpole stood out the storm.   What
was quite as important, though no effort was spared to
turn them against him, the king and queen held as firm
as the minister.   Lord Stair sought an audience of the
queen and assured her that Walpole was hated by the
army as a peace-man, by the clergy as a Whig, by the
city because he only regarded the great moneyed com-
panies, and he was hated by the Scotch because he
always showed that he hated them.   Unluckily, Stair
let fall something about his conscience.   " Oh, my lord,"
cried the queen, " don't talk to me of conscience; you will
make me faint."   She told him that his patriot strain
could move her to nothing but laughter; that he only
borrowed his politics and his professions from Bolingbroke and Carteret; and that he might, if he thought fit,
tell those lords that she had long known them to be two
as worthless men of parts as any in this country, and
long known them too, both by experience and report, to
be two of the greatest liars and knaves in any country.

Walpole expressed his readiness to resign at the very
first moment when either the king or the queen should
think that such a step would ease their business in Parliament.   The queen wondered how he could suppose her
to be so mean, cowardly, and ungrateful as to entertain
the offer for an instant; and the king declared that as the
minister had done all that could be done for the honour
and service of his master, that master would never forsake

him; they would stand or fall together. The king's own best quality was courage, and he admired the same quality in his minister. When Hervey told him of the encounters between Walpole and his enemies in the House of Commons, the king, he says, would often cry out, with colour flushing into his cheeks and tears sometimes in his eyes, and with a vehement oath, "*He is a brave fellow ; he has more spirit than any man I ever knew.*"

The minister, however, was much too wise to suppose that the fidelity of the court was enough to support him against the feeling of the country. He was neither a Strafford nor a North. Nor was he constitutional pedant enough to act as if the mere sanction of a majority in Parliament made a measure either expedient or safe. On the night when his majority had fallen to seventeen, he stood for some time after the House was up, leaning against the table with his hat pulled over his eyes, a few of his friends hanging with melancholy faces around him. He assembled a dozen of them to supper at his house. "*This dance,*" he said, "*will no further go.* I meant well, but in the present inflamed temper of the people, the Act could not be carried into execution without an armed force ; and there will be an end of the liberty of England if supplies are to be raised by the sword. If, therefore, the resolution is to proceed with the bill, I will instantly request the king's permission to resign, for I will not be the minister to enforce taxes at the expense of blood."

Accordingly the next day, when the order for the second reading of one of the Tobacco Bills was read, Walpole got up, and in a dexterous speech expressed his intention of postponing it for two months. This was understood to mean the abandonment of the scheme. The Opposition broke out into triumphant jubilation, and the wilder spirits could not restrain the fierceness of their satisfaction. Every night of these debates the Court of Requests, through which members passed on their way to and from the House, had been crowded with an excited throng, who cheered and hooted honourable gentlemen as they were known to have supported or opposed the hated excise. On this last night, when victory might have been expected to make them good-humoured, they were more violent than before, greeting every supporter of the minister with "ironical thanks, hissings, hallooings, and all other insults which it was possible to put upon them without proceeding to blows." Walpole's friends urged him to go out by another way, fearing that his great bulk would make it hard for him to run the gauntlet of the exasperated rioters without being trampled down. He persisted, however, and the tumult was so violent that but for the succour of Pelham and others of his friends he would hardly have escaped with his life.

The abandonment of the bill was the signal for boisterous and universal exultation that lasted for many days. The event was celebrated as if it had been a great victory over Frenchmen or Spaniards. Men went about with badges in their hats, bearing the very foolish inscription, *Liberty, Property, and No Excise.* The Monument was illuminated. Bonfires were lighted, and the rude mob, so well known to us from the ruthless pencil of Hogarth, flung into the flames with triumphant execrations the effigies of Sir Robert Walpole and a fat woman designed for Queen Caroline. At Oxford the com-

memoration of victorious folly was spiced with sanguine
treason.   In that famous home of so many bad causes,
for three nights together round the bonfires gownsmen
and townsmen drank openly to the good health of
Ormond, Bolingbroke, and King James the Third.   The
last note of the storm was heard more than twenty
years later, when Johnson in his dictionary defined excise
as " a hateful tax levied upon commodities, and adjudged
not by common judges of property, but by wretches
hired by those to whom excise is paid."

Walpole did not shrink from making the weight of his
resentment felt by some of those who held great posts
under the Crown, and yet had ventured to thwart the first
minister of the Crown.   As Lord Chesterfield was going
up the great staircase at St. James's he was summoned by
a messenger to the Duke of Grafton, who informed him of
the king's command that he should surrender his white
staff as Lord Steward.   Three other English peers were
dismissed from their offices in the household, and three
Scotch peers shared the same fate.   Even the holders of
military commands were as sharply treated as civilians.
As a rule, the king strove to retain the affairs of the army
in his own hands.   If Walpole asked for the smallest commission to oblige a member of Parliament, the king would
say, "I won't do it; you understand nothing of troops;
I will order my army as I think fit; for your scoundrels
of the House of Commons, you may do as you please;
you know I never interfere, or pretend to know anything
of them; but this province I will keep to myself."   On
the great occasion of the excise he allowed Walpole to
have his way.   Two high nobles, Lord Cobham, the
colonel of the king's regiment of horse, and the Duke of

Bolton, colonel of the king's regiment of guards, were both summarily deprived of their commands. Walpole is sometimes blamed for these high-handed proceedings. He is accused of dismissing Chesterfield, for instance, because Chesterfield had shown the two intolerable qualities of talent and independence. Such censure is really idle. So far as the civil appointments at any rate are concerned, Walpole only acted on a principle which is now part of the accepted foundation of Cabinet government, and without which nobody would to-day either form a government or expect to be a member of a government. Chesterfield openly grumbled against the excise bills, and privately made his brothers vote against them. He was at the head of the little group of peers who had long wished Walpole ill in secret, and who with many meetings, whisperings, and consultations had persuaded themselves that the hour had come for striking at him.[1] It is true that the bills were dropped, but what minister would have gone on with a colleague who had helped to force him to drop them? It hardly followed that because Walpole abandoned the old practice of cutting off an opponent's head, therefore he was bound to keep him in a Cabinet. A weak minister like Pelham would have overlooked any amount of disloyalty, but a strong minister like Chatham or Chatham's son would have acted as Walpole acted. The great moralist, we may notice, was on the side of Thorough. Dr. Johnson always declared that if he had been minister he would have done just what Walpole did. "If any man wagged his finger at me, he should be turned out. If you will not oppose at

---

[1] Hervey, ch. viii.

the risk of losing your place, your opposition cannot be honest."

Some have argued that Walpole was bound to persist in his scheme or to throw up the seals. It is a surprise to find a writer who united to literary splendour so much practical common sense as Macaulay, blaming Walpole for consenting in deference to popular opinion to abandon a measure which he thought in principle to be right. Peel, with the instinct of the debater, puts a crushing retort into Walpole's mouth; for Macaulay, though he admitted the corn law to be against principle, had recently (1833) declared himself for maintaining the corn law, simply because the constituencies were divided on the subject. "I at least," Peel makes Walpole reply, "tried the measure which I thought right. I did not abandon it until success was proved to be hopeless and opposition to be universal. But you my accuser, when you are in office, shrink from even the proposal of what you think right. On your own showing you find public opinion not unanimous against your measure, but equally divided as to its merits; and yet, with all justice and half the people on your side, you do that, without a struggle, which you consider it disgraceful for me to have done after the battle and after defeat." [1]

There is no doubt that Walpole could have carried the excise through Parliament. Only four of his men deserted to the enemy, and most of those who abstained on minor divisions would have come up to the mark on the main question. But the great parliamentary leader knew when it was wise to look beyond the walls of Parliament. It was the difficulty of executing

[1] Lord Stanhope's *Miscellanies* (1863), p. 80.

the Act, not of passing the Act, that made him yield.
He could have passed it, but he could not carry it out
without tumult and disorder. This is in itself a good
answer to the contention that he ought to have resigned. No minister is bound to resign so long as he
commands a parliamentary majority, though it may well
be held that he is bound to resign or dissolve if he has
reason to believe that the majority in Parliament does
not represent the constituencies. Sir Robert Peel resigned in the winter of 1845, because he believed that
the repeal of the duties on corn had become a pressing
necessity, and because he foresaw that he would break
up his party if he were to undertake the task. Walpole's circumstances in 1733 were quite different. He
knew that his fiscal policy was a wise policy, but it was
in no sense a national necessity. He knew that the
country could be perfectly well governed without an
excise on tobacco, and that to insist on an excise in the
face of strong popular opinion would be a piece of exceedingly bad government. Finally, he knew that his
resignation would be a grave mischief both to the king
and to the country, because it would hand over the
public interests to a motley band of ambitious men,
partly honest Tories, partly disloyal Jacobites, partly
malcontent Whigs, who had no common principles,
who had never shown any capacity for common action,
and who were now only united by common disappointment and malevolence.

Walpole's handling of the public debt varied with his
view of political emergencies, and, like the excise, has
exposed him to some censure. When he first came to
the Treasury (1717) the national debt stood at fifty-

four millions, bearing an average interest of between six and seven per cent. Walpole produced a plan for reducing the interest and establishing a sinking fund for the redemption of the principal.

Ten years later it appeared that the net result of the operation, when taken into account with new debts contracted, was a decrease of the debt by little more than two and a half millions. Walpole professed to adhere to the policy of the sinking fund, and he effected a further reduction of interest from five to four per cent. His virtue, however, did not endure much longer, for after various minor alienations he boldly proposed in 1733 to take half a million from the sinking fund for the service of the year, and he boldly gave the true reasons for this startling attack upon his own provision. He told Parliament that if they would not let him have the money in this way, he should have to raise the land tax from one to two shillings in the pound, and he did not deem it wise thus to increase the burdens that already pressed heavily enough on the landed interest. The sinking fund, " that sacred blessing and the nation's only hope," as some writers called it, was again and again invaded in each subsequent year, so that by the end of 1739, after seventeen years of profound peace, the whole sum paid off was no more than £8,328,000, leaving a capital debt just short of £47,000,000. [1]

If Walpole had been an extravagant minister, and had used for excessive expenditure the funds that might have lightened the load on the next generation, his action would have been without excuse. But no financier was ever more thrifty of the national resources. His

[1] See *Wealth of Nations*, bk. v. ch. iii.

motive was political, and in critical times fiscal maxims
will always be rightly qualified and governed by political requirements.   To bring the Hanoverian Government into favour with the landed men was, as has often
been said, one of the cardinal points in Walpole's whole
policy and in every part of it.   But in laying hands
upon the sinking fund, or, in other words, in suspending
the payment of debt, he was gratifying two other interests as well.   He pleased the fundholders, who did
not wish to have their money thrown on their hands
when they had no other secure investments open.   He
pleased the general taxpayer, who is never unwilling to
let his masters shift a burden forward on to the shoulders
of future generations.

The same considerations of general policy explain
Walpole's resistance in 1737 to a proposal made by Sir
John Barnard for reducing the interest on the national
debt to three per cent, and the compulsory redemption of
certain annuities existing at a higher rate.   At first
Walpole wavered, and his final decision against the plan
was evidently the result of close observation of public
opinion, and calculation of the strength of the opposing
interests.   The whole number of persons affected by
the proposal was 23,000; of these, 6000 were executors
or trustees for widows and orphans, and more than
17,000 were proprietors of sums not exceeding one
thousand pounds.   To this large class the reduction of
their income by one-fourth would be a serious distress
and embarrassment.   The minister had a stronger
reason for not wounding the moneyed interest.   He
foresaw the too probable approach of an early war with
Spain, and he knew how great would be the advantage

in that emergency of having the men with money to lend in a good humour, and of keeping the public faith with the creditors even more punctiliously than strict legality required.

Even those who blame Walpole for what they regard as a selfish and timid sacrifice of the real interests of the country to personal convenience, admit that the public debt might be viewed as a pillar of the Hanoverian Government. The notion that the Pretender, if he came into his own again, would repudiate a debt contracted to keep him out of his own, obviously made every fund-holder a zealous partisan of the existing establishment. It was in vain that Jacobites protested that the *Spectator's* vision of James with a flaming sword in one hand and a sponge in the other, was a vile Whig calumny.[1] The public creditor pinned his faith on Walpole, and Walpole took care that he should have good grounds for his faith. For many years the public conviction was as strong as that of George I., that Walpole could make gold from nothing, and anticipated the later judgment of economic writers that Walpole was the greatest commercial minister that this country had then ever seen.

[1] See Lord Stanhope's *History of England*, ch. xvi. p. 158, 5th ed.

CHAPTER IX

FOREIGN historians sometimes talk of the torpor of the Walpolean era. Doubtless the era had none of the glory of Elizabeth, or Cromwell, or Chatham. Yet it was now that the bearers of two of the most illustrious names in the literary history of the century came to kindle in England the lamp of European illumination. Voltaire visited this country in 1726, and Montesquieu followed him hither in 1732. It was Walpole's England that inspired the *Philosophic Letters* and the *Spirit of Laws*. The violence of faction, the froth of parliamentary passion, the boisterous humours of elections, did not divert these brilliant and sincere observers from the truth of the matter. They felt the movement, the freedom, the full pulse and current of vitality, under an uninteresting surface. The fact that Voltaire deemed most worthy of attention under the head of government was equality of taxation. The contrast between England and France was a poignant one to his humane and social intelligence. "Here," he said, "the peasant has not his feet bruised by sabots, he eats white bread, he is well clad, he is not afraid of increasing the number of his cattle or putting tiles on his house, lest next

year he should have his taxes raised." He noticed
with amazement and admiration that in England the
younger son of a peer did not disdain to carry on useful
business in the city, while in France he would have
scorned any life outside the frivolous slavery of Versailles. Though the government was in the hands of
an aristocratic oligarchy, the oligarchy was not a caste.
Later economists believe that the earnings of the
labourer have not for many ages commanded so large
a portion of subsistence as at this period of the eighteenth
century. Hallam, like Malthus, is of opinion that, in
respect of the real happiness of the community, the
reign of George II might be advantageously compared
with the more brilliant but less steady condition of later
times.[1]

One of the grand articles against Walpole is, that
though he was at the head of affairs for so many
years, not one great measure, not one important change
for better or worse marks the period of his supremacy.
He ought, according to Whigs of our day, to have
shortened the duration of Parliaments; yet all the wisest
of the reforming Whigs of that and the next generation
held that more frequent elections would be an aggrava-
tion of every parliamentary mischief. He ought to
have insisted on limiting the number of placemen and
excluding pensioners; yet when the innovators set to
work in 1780 they judiciously sought for a real remedy,
not in the exclusion of placemen, but the suppression of
places. The patriots who had clamoured against Walpole's corruption for twenty years, tolerated, practised, and
aggravated every evil of his system for twenty years after.

[1] *Constitutional History*, ch. xvi. 3, 302, 10th ed.

Before they blame Walpole for not introducing great measures and making important changes, his critics ought to say for what important change the time was ripe and the opportunity safe. A vast and important change had been made at the accession of the Hanoverian line. The one object of a wise minister was not to make other changes, but to guard that. Some ministers are great because they pass great measures, others because they either prepare or secure them. Walpole was a great minister of the second of these two orders. Why should we mete out to him a measure which nobody applies to other statesmen of his commanding position? Walpole has rather a bad character and the younger Pitt has an exceedingly good one : so Walpole is condemned as selfish and unprincipled for not being a reformer and not helping the dissenters, while Mr. Pitt stands undisturbed on his pedestal, though he spoke against meddling with the Test Act, though he allowed parliamentary reform, which he had taken up in opposition, to drop when he was in power, and though he solemnly abandoned Catholic emancipation after as solemnly treating it as a condition of a great international compact. In saying this, I am not judging Pitt, but offering a standard by which we may judge Walpole.

Political tranquillity was a condition of material advance. Under the appearance of torpor, men were minding their business, and preparing the ways and means for that immense expansion which we associate with the name and policy of Chatham. Taxes were light; public credit was high; the administration of justice, which, after taxation, is the most important branch of government for the happiness of a people, was,

on the whole, upright, equal, and sure.   Even in the
spiritual sphere, historians of thought have been justified
in asking whether in the first half of the nineteenth
century we could find three bishops of higher purity and
devotion than Berkeley, Butler, and Wilson; divines
more honest and manly than Clarke, or with a finer glow
of devout sentiment than Law; workers of more honourable and laborious life than Watt, Lardner, and Dodd-
ridge, who all of them sacrificed preferment to conscience.[1]

The dissenters, it is true, still laboured under disabili-
ties.   The bills against occasional conformity and in
restraint of the rights of dissenters to educate their
children had been repealed in 1719 (*ante*, p. 55).   A
motion for the repeal of the Test Act was thrown out
in 1736 by Walpole's advice.   As the dissenters were
peaceful and law-abiding, and gave him no trouble, he
would run no risk for their sake, and the Sacheverell
explosion had taught him how sharp and serious the
risk might be.   All this is true enough, but it would
have been little less than madness in any statesman,
for a generation at least, to forget for a day the lesson of
the Sacheverell explosion.   That extraordinary outbreak had led to the Tory Government of the last four
years of Queen Anne, and—to use again a strong expression that I have borrowed before—nothing short
of the greatest miracle in our history prevented the
Tory Government of the last four years of Anne ending
either in a legitimist restoration or a civil war.   A
statesman who had seen the constitution come so close
as that to disaster, might well think it better that the

---

[1] See Mr. Leslie Stephen's *English Thought in the Eighteenth
Century*, ii. 384.

dissenters should continue for some time longer to endure harsh laws, than that new provocation to the Church should bring back the old peril to the State.

Three years later the dissenters again approached Walpole, urging the repeal of the Test Act. He gave them the reply, so well known from all ministers to all reformers, that he quite agreed with them, but that the time was not opportune. One of the deputation hardily asked him when the time would come. "If you want a specific answer," said Walpole, "I will give it you in a single word—Never." But reparation was made by the Indemnity Act, first passed in the first year of George II, and renewed every year afterwards, with three or four interruptions, down to 1828, when the sacramental test disappeared. The test remained, to please the pride of Churchmen, but if a dissenter chose to break it with certain not unimportant limitations, he could evade the penalty. The struggle against occasional conformity had been inspired, not merely by dislike of religious toleration, but by the solid political object of closing to dissenters the corporations which returned members of Parliament. Walpole's policy as to tests secured the practical victory, while leaving the obnoxious flag of church privilege still flying. Lord Chancellor Cowper informed George I. on his accession that, if the clergy could be brought round, all differences of opinion as to the royal title would soon vanish among the laity. This extraordinary and dangerous authority would undoubtedly have been exerted against the parliamentary constitution, as the authority of clericalism has been in France, if Walpole had roused latent passions. The closing of the doors of Convocation in 1717 was an effective protest against the virulence of ecclesiastical controversy, and no other was ever demanded.

Early in his career, Walpole had encountered the obduracy of Scottish sentiment. In 1725 the disgust of the English country gentlemen at the exemption of Scotland from the duty on malt, had grown so clamorous as to force him to propose a sixpenny tax on every barrel of ale brewed in Great Britain. The Scots took fire. All the dialectic ingenuity of the race was invoked against the obnoxious sixpence. The transfer of the duty on malt to a duty on beer was contrary to the Act of Union : now the violation of any material article of a compact is a legal dissolution of the whole : therefore the Union was dissolved. But the dissolution of the Union revived the Scottish Act of 1681. Therefore King George was no longer entitled to Scottish allegiance, and the next in succession of the Stuart line became King of Scotland. This train of argument was decorated with references to the separation of Denmark from Sweden, to the rejection of the yoke of Spain by the United Provinces, and to the revolt of Israel from Judah. The Scots had resisted the oppressions of Charles II and James VII : should they not now resist the tyrannical minister who had rivetted chains upon his king and his country ?

Violent tumults broke out in Glasgow and other towns. The troops were called in, and there was considerable loss of life. The Edinburgh brewers entered into a solemn compact that they would rather not brew than pay the duty. The government held firm. Proceedings were instituted against the brewers for payment of the duty on stock in hand. They were told

that nothing would be listened to, short of entire submission. They met to discuss the question, *Brew or not
brew?* The chairman began to take the votes on his
right hand; but the right-hand man thought it hard
upon him to have to speak first, and the left-hand man
thought the same, and nobody would be the first to
speak. At length one man plucked up courage to vote
Brew, and by noon the next day, says Walpole, forty
brewhouses were hard at work in Edinburgh and ten
more in Leith. This satisfactory result was due to
the firmness and judgment of Lord Islay. The Duke
of Roxburgh, then Secretary of State for Scotland and
a friend of Carteret, had secretly encouraged resistance
by representations that the days of Walpole's power
were numbered. The minister sent prompt remonstrances to the king, and Roxburgh was compelled to
resign.

The circumstances of the Porteous riot are familiar
wherever the English tongue is spoken, because they
were made the dramatic opening of one of his finest
stories by that admirable genius who, like Shakespeare in
his plays, has conveyed to plain men more of the spirit
and action of the past in noble fiction, than they would
find in most professed chronicles of fact. The early
scenes of the *Heart of Midlothian* are an accurate account
of the transaction which gave so much trouble to Queen
Caroline and the minister. A smuggler who had excited
the popular imagination by his daring and his chivalry
was sentenced to be hanged; after his execution the mob
pressed forward to cut down his body: Porteous, the
captain of the City Guard, ordered his men to fire, and
several persons were shot dead : he was tried for murder,

convicted, and sentenced, but at the last moment a reprieve arrived from London, to the intense indignation of a crowd athirst for vengeance : four days later, under mysterious ringleaders who could never afterwards be discovered, fierce throngs suddenly gathered together at nightfall to the beat of drum, broke into the prison, dragged out the unhappy Porteous, and sternly hanged him on a dyer's pole close by the common place of public execution.

Carteret thought that these wild doings furnished good material for a parliamentary attack (1737). If the government did nothing, he could denounce them for indifference to law and order. If they took sharp measures, he knew that it would kindle the resentment of the Scotch. In either case, moreover, he would discredit the authority of Lord Islay, to whom the minister looked for the management of Scotch affairs. This calculation proved quite correct. Walpole was bound to cover Lord Islay, as well as his brother the Duke of Argyle, and he dreaded lest the affair should become national. The Lord Provost of Edinburgh and four bailies were summoned to the bar of the House of Lords, and it at once became evident that so far as feeling in Scotland went, the affair was already national in its full extent. Their testimony showed that ninety-nine Scotchmen out of every hundred thought that Porteous had been justly condemned, and justly put to death. Islay warned Walpole that any attempt to inflict excessive punishment for Porteous's murder, would make the whole of Scotland disaffected, and would render the government of the country impossible.

In the course of a prolonged and acrimonious controversy the Scottish judges were examined at the bar of the House of Lords ; and a bill of pains and penalties was brought in for disqualifying the Provost of Edinburgh for all magisterial office in Great Britain ; inflicting on him a term of imprisonment ; abolishing the Town Guard of the city ; and removing the gates of the Nether Bow Port. This stringent bill passed the House of Lords by a majority of fifty-four to twenty-two. On reaching the Commons it immediately encountered very rude treatment. The forty-five Scottish members, regarding the bill as an insult to their nation, were against it to a man. The Tories professed to be opposed on principle to all bills of pains and penalties. Things began to look as if the bill would be flung out, and all Walpole's tact was required to prevent a parliamentary disaster. After a heated conflict the imprisonment of the Provost was dropped, and so were the clauses for disbanding the Town Guard and demolishing the town gate. In their stead a provision was inserted, imposing a fine of two thousand pounds on the Corporation for the benefit of Porteous's widow. The generality of mankind, says Hervey, looking on these great transactions in cold blood, were not a little amused at Parliament spending five months in declaring that a man should never again be a magistrate who had never wished to be one, and in raising two thousand pounds on the city of Edinburgh, to make the widow of Captain Porteous with unconjugal joy bless the hour in which her husband was hanged.

The course of these affairs contains the best answer to the charge, made by Macaulay among others, that it was the obvious and pressing duty of a British statesman to break the power of the Highland chiefs,

and that it was through Walpole's failure to regulate
the Highlands in a time of peace, that his successors were
forced to conquer them in the middle of a war with
France and Spain. In 1738 Duncan Forbes, the acute
and well-informed President of the Court of Session,
submitted a scheme for raising four or five thousand
men in the Highlands; the disaffected districts would
thus be drained; the pride of the chiefs would be
gratified by the bestowal of his Majesty's commission;
and active military life would please the martial tastes
of the clansmen. Walpole saw what was to be gained,
and approved generally of the scheme.[1] Two considerations of different degrees of weight made him hesitate.
One was the clamour, always very loud, and just then
particularly likely to rise to its stormiest pitch, against
a standing army. The other and stronger argument
was the intense national sentiment of Scotland, so
vividly shown in the recent affair of Porteous, and the
certainty that the levy of a large Highland force by
order of the government, would undoubtedly have been
represented as a design on the national freedom. On
these grounds, we hold that Walpole was right in leaving
the Highlands alone. What was easy for Pitt, after all
fear of the Stuarts had practically come to an end, and
after the spirit of partisanship and intrigue had died out
of the Highlands, even if it was not actually impossible
in Walpole's time, would without dispute have been
extremely dangerous.

The resentment of Scotland could not make itself felt
before the arrival of a general election, which was still
four years off. Meanwhile Walpole was suddenly con-

[1] *The Culloden Papers*, p. xxxi.

fronted with formidable and pressing peril nearer home.
The smouldering hatred within the royal family burst
out in a fierce explosion in 1737. Walpole described
this unnatural conflict as the most troublesome and the
most dangerous he had yet known. It arose from the
marriage of the Prince of Wales, and was destined to
have in the fulness of time a disastrous effect on the
fortunes of Walpole. Prince Frederick, like his grandson George IV, is a striking instance of the common and
inevitable contrast in courts between important position
and paltry character. By placing himself at the head
of the able band in opposition, he took the sting out
of Walpole's standing charge, that the coalition was
essentially Jacobite ; and the adhesion of the heir to
the throne marked a signal change in the position of
Pulteney, Wyndham, Carteret, and their friends. The
prince was vain, childish, and truthless. In 1745, when
the news arrived that the Highland rebels had reached
Derby, and that his brother had marched northward to
meet them, he was found playing at blindman's buff
with the pages. He had a passion for disguising himself
and running off to bull-baits at Hockley-in-the-Hole.
He was incontinent of speech, heedless of all correspondence between words and things, and while overflowing
with conceit, was destitute of self-respect. This was the
material out of which Bolingbroke designed to make his
first Patriot King.

The prince, on his marriage, found his allowance
of 50,000*l.* not enough for his new establishment. It
was, moreover, intensely galling to him to feel that
even this sum was not permanently settled by the
arrangement of Parliament, but took the form of an

annual gratuity from his father. To have too little
money was bad enough, but to owe even a meagre
income to the goodwill of a man whom he hated, was
unbearable. Bolingbroke and Chesterfield were at his
ear, with the sinister counsel that he should bring his
irksome situation to an end by boldly laying his case
before Parliament. If Parliament could be induced to
request the king to settle 100,000*l.* a year on the prince,
with a jointure on the princess, then he would have
gained three grand objects : he would have acquired a
proper income, secured his own emancipation, and mortally
vexed his father. The news that the prince had fallen in
with this suggestion, exasperated the court beyond all control. The queen a hundred times a day cursed the hour in
which her eldest son had been born, and a hundred times
a day she and the Princess Caroline wished that he
might drop down dead of an apoplexy. The angry
fires did not burn any the less furiously from the
apprehension that the prince might carry Parliament
with him. Lists made out by his own friends promised
him a majority of forty, and even the minister's list
could not bring it lower than ten. Walpole took serious
alarm. He saw that the moderate people, on whom he
always relied, felt the injustice of leaving the princess
without a jointure, and the prince a pensioner at pleasure
on the king. Accordingly, with much difficulty, he persuaded the king to send his son a message, promising a
jointure and a settled allowance of 50,000*l.* He knew
the risk he ran, in the inflamed state of mind of his
royal masters, of rousing the shadow of a suspicion that
he was currying favour with the prince. " But it is
my way, you know," he said to Hervey, " and when you

come to be in my place, I advise you to make it your way too, to provide against the present difficulty that presses." He could make the best of the royal jealousies another day. Meanwhile, the prince shuffled, begged the ministers who conveyed the message to him to lay him at his majesty's feet, to assure his majesty of his utmost duty for the royal person, and of his sense of the royal goodness and graciousness; but that the affair was now out of his hands, and he could give no answer.

The king was more enraged than ever, and roughly reproached Walpole for subjecting him to such a repulse. Walpole answered that the good he expected from the proceeding was to be reaped to-morrow, not to-day; and that what he had proposed by it was to bring the House of Commons to reason, not the Prince of Wales. When Pulteney brought on the motion for an address begging the king to settle 100,000*l.* a year on the heir-apparent, Walpole replied in a speech of singular firmness and address. After a long debate, the motion was lost by a handsome majority of thirty against it. It was commonly supposed to have cost the court a great deal of money in bribing members of Parliament, and the king, though delighted with the result, grumbled at the amount. Yet it appears that the cost, after all, did not exceed 900*l.*, in two sums of 500*l.* and 400*l.* respectively, to two gentlemen who were to have received the money at the end of the session in any case, and who only took advantage of this particular occasion to exact prompt payment. This is the one definite case of direct parliamentary bribery in Walpole's history.

"If ever any man in any cause," said Walpole afterwards, "fought dagger out of sheath, I did so in the

House of Commons that day." He knew that he carried
his political life in his hand. If he leaned ever so
slightly towards the prince, he ruined himself with the
king and queen. If he defied the prince, he ruined
himself with the man who might be king to-morrow.
The king, as it happened, had barely recovered from a
serious illness, and to people in the lively and morbid
expectancy that is natural to all oppositions, it seemed
that he might disappear any day. Bolingbroke expressed his amazement at Walpole's imprudence. In
truth Walpole knew very well what he was about. He
acted on the maxims which had been the key to his
success. He had recognised what was just in the
prince's demand. By conceding it he had put his
opponents in the wrong. He averted the actual and
present difficulty with the king, without regard to the
contingency of future difficulties with the prince. When
we hear of the mischief of a system which makes great
ministers responsible to the public opinion of democracy,
it is well to remember the embarrassments and dangers
that beset great ministers from the private passions of
a court.

The miscarriage of the project that was to have done
such fine things for him, made it all the more odious to
the prince to have to live under the same roof with his
detested parents at Hampton Court or at St. James's.
He attended drawingrooms and levées, and dined with
the court in public; but the queen, though she allowed
him to take her hand, never spoke to him, and the king
pretended to be wholly unconscious of his presence.
The prince suddenly brought things to a violent crisis.
One night (1737), while the royal family were at

Hampton Court, the princess was seized with the pains
of labour.   She was hurried into a chaise and driven off
at the risk of her life at full gallop to St. James's,
where in less than an hour after her arrival, the unfortunate lady was delivered.   The queen was roused at
one in the morning with the news of the flight; she
instantly dressed, ordered coaches, hurried after the
singular fugitives, and by four found herself at St.
James's at the bedside of her daughter-in-law.   The
king's fury at his son's escapade knew no bounds.
Scoundrel and puppy, knave and fool, liar and coward,
were on his lips at every moment.   It was all Walpole's
fault, for forcing his master to settle 50,000*l.* a year on
the ingrate, and so make him independent for life.

Walpole took the royal storm with his usual composure.   At the same time he knew very well that the
feud between the king and the prince was also a struggle
between himself and the Opposition.   The prince was
nothing without Carteret and Pulteney, Bolingbroke
and Chesterfield.   Some of his own colleagues, too, were
less intrepid than himself.   They were less disposed
than he was to burn their boats, to cut off all hopes
of future honour and emolument, and Lord Hardwicke
especially remonstrated against the asperity of the
message by which the king turned his son out of
doors.   This only made Walpole more determined to
hold to his own course against prince, opposition,
and trimming colleagues.   The Chancellor, the Duke
of Newcastle, and others who were of the same
mind, were for giving the prince another chance
of making his submission.   No, said Walpole, there
is nothing like taking it "short at first."   The prince

was ordered instantly to quit St. James's Palace, and
he borrowed the Duke of Norfolk's house in St. James's
Square. The guard was taken away from his door.
There was even an ignoble squabble as to the articles of
furniture which he had a right to carry with him. The
foreign ministers were informed that it would be agree-
able to the king if they abstained from visiting the
prince. A written message was even sent to all peers,
peeresses, and privy councillors, that if they went to the
prince's court they would be excluded from the king's
presence. The prince was not to wait many years for
revenge. As we shall see, when the critical moment
arrived, he became the principal agent in depriving the
king of his minister, and driving Walpole from power.

The heaviest blow in Walpole's ministerial career
followed these vexatious events. In the winter of 1737
Queen Caroline died. From an excess of delicacy
remarkable in one of her strong character, and only to
be accounted for by the peculiar nature of her relations
with her husband, she concealed from her physicians an
infirmity with which she had for some years been
afflicted. They pursued an erroneous course of treatment, and when they discovered her secret it was too
late. She met her end with serenity and fortitude.
One unnatural antipathy burnt fiercely to the end; the
clergy made her profess forgiveness of her eldest son,
but to the last she refused to see him. The king hovered
incessantly about her bedside, sometimes blubbering and
maudlin, sometimes bullying and peevish. No more
extraordinary death-bed conversation can ever have
taken place between husband and wife. The dying
queen urged him to marry again. Wiping his eyes,

and his voice choked by sobs, he ejaculated, "*Non, j'aurai des maîtresses.*"—"*Ah, mon Dieu !*" replied the queen, "*cela n'empêche pas.*" When Walpole arrived the king took him to the bedside. The queen said: "My good Sir Robert, you see me in a very indifferent situation. I have nothing to say to you, but to recommend the king, and my children, and the kingdom to your care."

The change in Walpole's position was profound, and everybody was sensible of it and acted upon it. "Though he may have more power with the king than any other body," said the shrewd Chesterfield, "yet he will never have that kind of power which he had by her means, and he will never dare to mention many things to the king, which he would without difficulty have brought about by her means."[1] Newcastle and the Chancellor were even emboldened to talk to the king on their own account. The difficulty of managing the House of Commons was increased by the rise in the demands of his followers of the baser sort, in proportion to his greater need for them. The resentment of the heir to the throne for the affronts that Walpole had put upon him, became keener as he saw a nearer chance of gratifying it. All this only brings into stronger relief the bluff courage with which Walpole, now left standing absolutely alone, confronted the fury of Opposition, the selfishness of colleagues, and the sudden humours of the king.

[1] 12th November 1737, v. 427.

CHAPTER X

FOREIGN POLICY

IT is a misfortune for the popularity of Walpole's reputation that the most important chapter in his policy should have become in its details the least interesting. Even the vivid genius of Carlyle could not bring to life again the European diplomacy of the eighteenth century. Congresses without issue, campaigns without visible objective, open treaties, secret articles, public alliances, private combinations, the destruction to-day of the web laboriously woven yesterday, the union of four powers against one, of three against two, and so on in every possible variety of permutation and combination, make a vast chaos in comparison with which even the perturbed Europe of to-day is a scene of stability and order. Towards the close of Walpole's rule momentous issues for Great Britain and for mankind arose on the blurred horizon of continental struggles in diplomacy and the field. Until that time Walpole's guiding principle was to hold England back from European strife.

Peace was indispensable to the success of his policy. It was essential alike to material development and political consolidation. War meant high expenditure

and a land tax at four shillings, whereas he sought to
reconcile the landed men to the new settlement by
keeping the land tax low. War was an interruption of
that energetic devotion to trade and manufacture
which was so remarkable a sign of the time, and which
was every year adding enormously to the wealth and
strength of the country. In case of war our enemy
would assuredly launch the Pretender and rouse the
Jacobites, if not in England, at any rate in Scotland.
War, in fine, would certainly at an earlier or later stage
come to be associated in the public mind with the
Hanoverian connection, and the burdens of war would
become so many arguments against the dynasty. For
all these cogent reasons, peace has never been so
imperative an object to Great Britain as it was for the
generation after Utrecht.

Townshend advanced a certain way in the path of
non-intervention, but not on principle or system. To
Walpole belongs the chief credit of perceiving that the
time had come for altering the foreign policy of his
party. The Whigs had supported King William in his
vast schemes of continental alliances and campaigns.
Year after year they had placed all the resources of England at the disposal of Marlborough. They had denounced
and resisted the Peace of Utrecht, and with every circumstance of passion and animosity had impeached its authors.
With Walpole new maxims definitely arose within the
Whig party. Principles of peace, of neutrality, of diplomacy as a substitute for war, began slowly to find favour
among them. Walpole did not carry the whole of the
party with him in his new departure; and if here were
the proper place it would be interesting to trace this

great line of division between the two sections of Whigs
down to the end of the century; to show how the
differences between Walpole and Sunderland were
reproduced between Walpole and Carteret; how the
tradition of the Sunderland Whigs was carried on by
the elder Pitt, and from him descended to Shelburne;
how it was opposed by Burke and the Rockingham
Whigs—the representatives of Walpole's policy with
loftier phrases and a deeper morality—how it helps to
explain the quarrels between Shelburne and Fox; how
the younger Pitt, who so long looked on himself as a
Whig, acted mainly on Walpolean maxims, until Burke
flung them over under the stress of the French Revolution and compelled Pitt to do the same.

At the beginning of this great change in the policy of
his party, neither Walpole nor any other minister could
have carried it forward to a logical end. Absolute non-
intervention was impracticable. The king's Hanoverian
dominions involved us in Germany, as well in the affairs of
both Russia and Sweden in the north. The retention of
Gibraltar involved us for many years with Spain. Our
commerce with Spanish dependencies was the most extensive branch of British trade. The emperor's diplomacy
was expressly directed against our commercial marine.
Finally, we were still under the general obligations of
Utrecht. British interests in European affairs were
therefore direct, active, and substantial.

On the other side, in estimating the state of Europe,
the minister saw the continent distracted by the plots
and counterplots of ambitious and unscrupulous rulers
at Vienna and Madrid. He saw Russia beginning to
use her new ascendancy in the north against the

declining power of Sweden and Denmark. Holland was
slowly losing, and Prussia was surely gaining, a position
Caroline wittily observed of the Triple Alliance of 1735,
of decisive prominence.   Hardly a pretence of public
right guarded the state system of Europe.   What Queen
was equally true of the other combinations of the age.
It always put her in mind, she said, of the South Sea
scheme; people went into it knowing that it was all a
cheat, still hoping to get something out of it; everybody
meaning when he had made his own fortune to be the
first in scrambling away, and each thinking himself
sharp enough to be able to leave his fellow-adventurers
in the lurch.

When George I. in 1723 requested Walpole to
provide funds for operations against the Czar in his
attempt to depose the king of Sweden, the minister
found the money, but hoped that it might never be
wanted. "*My politics*," he said, "*are to keep free from all
engagements as long as we possibly can.*" Engagements
were inevitable.   No wide and comprehensive settlement of Europe was possible.   For us no standing
system of foreign policy was possible.   It was an epoch
of transition; too late to found a European policy on
religion, too early to found it on nationality; the
dynastic struggle which had raged for so many years
was coming to an end; the struggle for trade and the
new world was beginning.   It was no time for ambitious
general views, and Walpole was not the man to bewilder
himself, either by fictitious contingencies or by any of
the wild schemes that fascinated the rash and erratic
genius of Carteret.   It would be absurd to ascribe to
him any of those great ideals of European peace which

had inspired men in the fourteenth century, and were soon in new forms to revive in the superior speculative minds of the eighteenth. He had none of those high dreams of the universal mediator and peacemaker which men had hoped to realise first in the papacy, and then in the holy Roman empire, and which was now in the second of these august institutions so terribly miscarrying. Walpole was a man not of ideals, but of expedients, as the commander of an army in a campaign is a man of expedients. He looked at each crisis as it arose, from the point of the actual, positive, direct, and particular interests of England; and the one general view that he permitted himself was the wise and noble one that England's best interest lay in European peace.

The only hope for European peace lay in an alliance between England and France. Circumstances for the time made these two powers the mediators and peacemakers of Europe. The policy of Wolsey, of Elizabeth when she acted with Henry IV, of Cromwell when he acted with Mazarin, was reproduced by Walpole's alliance with Cardinal Fleury. Walpole probably did not very well know, and certainly did not at all care, what had been done by Wolsey, Elizabeth, or Cromwell; but he renewed their tradition, and by union with France, from his first entry into real power down to the second Treaty of Vienna in 1731, he secured for Europe intervals of peace in a period of extraordinary confusion and danger. The co-operation with Fleury was not always equally close, its aspect varied with the passing circumstances, it was always guarded, qualified, cautious, suspicious, it was often informal and unsystematic, occasionally it gave way; but it was strong enough and per-

sistent enough to produce a certain amount of rough and
practical peace, and it presents one of the most remarkable, satisfactory, and instructive pictures in the modern
history of Europe.[1]   Here again Walpole departed from
the old tradition of his own party.   It was enough to
make King William's Whigs turn in their grave, that
the influence of George I. should have procured a
cardinal's hat for a prime minister of France ; that the
British ambassador should be concerting military plans
at Versailles with Marshal Berwick, the son of King
James ; and that a serious proposal should come to
King George to allow his eldest daughter to turn
Catholic and marry Louis XV.

Between 1725 and 1731 the positions of Spain and
the Empire underwent incessant change.   The congress
of Cambrai had long been sitting under the auspices of
Great Britain and France as mediators, to compose the
differences arising out of their rivalry.   Europe was
suddenly informed that the rivals had composed their
own differences and made the Treaty of Vienna (1725).
The emperor, Spain, and Russia drew themselves up
in line against the rest of Europe.   England's direct
concern lay in certain secret articles that were alleged
to exist, by which Spain was to be supported in attack-
ing Gibraltar, the emperor to be supported in the Ostend
Company and his other maritime and commercial designs, and the Pretender to be supported by the Empire,
Spain, and Russia.   The immediate retort to the Treaty
of Vienna was the Treaty of Hanover (September 1725)
between England, France, and Prussia.   This combina-

[1] For the French view of Walpole's influence over Fleury, see
St. Simon, xv. 325 (ed. 1874).

tion was for many years bitterly attacked by the pamph-
leteers and orators of the Opposition. The very name of
the treaty enabled them to represent it as a sacrifice of
England to the German electorate. It was in truth to
expose the electorate for the sake of England. Walpole
himself, though he defended the Treaty of Hanover in
Parliament, doubted whether Townshend's apprehensions
were not exaggerated, and, looking to the quarter in
which it was his characteristic habit to look, he doubted
whether the House of Commons would willingly grant
the subsidies. The dispatch of a squadron to the Baltic
convinced Russia that the new allies were in earnest,
and it arrested mischief in the north. In the south Spain
opened the siege of Gibraltar, the emperor got his
forces together, Prussia fell away from the allies of
Hanover, and a general conflagration became imminent.
Only the prudence of Walpole and the good faith of Fleury
prevented it. A British expedition was sent to the Spanish
West Indies, but the admiral had instructions not to act
on the offensive. The allies were ready to assist us
against the Spanish attack, but Walpole insisted on
delay, and begged them to wait. We may almost
wonder even in our own enlightened day, how a minister could dare to be so sensible as Walpole. Though
this resolute tardiness in recourse to arms exposed him
to taunts of pusillanimity then and since, he was speedily
justified by the event. Within a few months the emperor,
finding himself without any of the outside support on
which he had reckoned, withdrew from his engagements
with Spain, the Treaty of Vienna fell to pieces, and, as a
result of the mediation of France, the preliminaries of
peace were signed by the emperor with England, France,

and Holland (1727). The death of George I. and the hopes which that event, and the expected fall of Walpole as a consequence, inspired in the enemies of England, caused some delay in ratifying the preliminaries, and it was not until after a period of dangerous suspense that in the spring of 1729 Great Britain, France, and Spain executed the Treaty of Seville. To England various commercial rights were restored which had been invaded by the Treaty of Vienna in 1725. Gibraltar was not mentioned. The charter of the Ostend Company was to be suspended. Spain was to be allowed under guarantees to introduce a force into Tuscany and Parma, as a security that the succession in these two provinces should revert to Don Carlos. The Treaty of Seville thus made a useful peace in one quarter, but, so complex and intricate was the game, it was a provocation to war in another. It left the emperor isolated and resentful, disappointed alike in his dynastic schemes and his imperial claims. Walpole, who was now free by the resignation of Townshend to pursue his own views, immediately addressed himself to Vienna. Without consulting Fleury, he proposed to the emperor to guarantee the succession of his daughter to the hereditary dominions of the House of Hapsburg in return for the abolition of the Ostend Company, and for the imperial assent to the entry of the Spanish troops into Parma. The emperor, to whom the succession of Maria Theresa had long been the main object of his life, came in to these terms, and after some difficulties in connection with the electorate of Hanover had been boldly thrust aside by Walpole for future arrangement, his grand plan was finally accepted in the second Treaty of Vienna in 1731. The European explosion was once more postponed.

None of these arduous transactions show Walpole's
difficulties more instructively than those which arose
out of the vacancy of the crown of Poland in 1733.
The events themselves are dead, but they show Walpole's method at its best.   His ends were wise, his
diplomatic management was penetrating and skilful,
and his union of tact and patience with immovable determination is a standing lesson in political action.   On
the death of the king of Poland a violent struggle
instantly began for the choice of a successor.   France
supported Stanislaus, the father of the French king's
consort, already once the wearer of the uneasy Polish
crown.   The emperor favoured Augustus, the elector
of Saxony, and son of the late king.   Russia took sides
with Austria, and Spain joined France.   Stanislaus suddenly appeared in the midst of the turbulent nobles, and
was hailed king by acclamation; Russia at once sent an
armed force into Warsaw.   Stanislaus took to flight,
and the partisans of Augustus elected him in triumph.
France, Spain, and Sardinia immediately declared war
against the emperor as instigator of the Russian attack.
By the beginning of 1734 Spain had made herself mistress of his possessions in southern Italy, Russia was of
little avail, and in his straits he addressed importunate
appeals to England.   The success of the operations
against the emperor had raised wider issues than the
difference between a French and an Austrian nominee
on the Polish throne.   Was Great Britain to see her
ancient ally beaten and stripped by England's ancient
enemies, French and Spanish Bourbons?   Was there not
good ground to suspect a Family Compact?   Was Great
Britain to watch with indifference such a derangement

of the balance of power in Europe as must inevitably
follow, if the war went on and the emperor were left to his
fate? George II answered questions of this kind by
vehement declarations in favour of succouring the emperor. He was a German and hated the French. As
elector of Hanover he was part and member of the
Empire, and bound to its head. His martial passion
always flamed out at the prospect of war. The emperor
offered his vanity an almost irresistible temptation by
actually proposing to place him in command of the
imperial army on the Rhine.

The queen's German sympathies drew her towards
the same views. Most of the Cabinet were with the
king. Newcastle used as big words as his master about
driving the Spaniards out of Italy and humbling the
pride of France. Lord Grantham reiterated his policy
in the simple creed, "I hate the French, and I hope as
we shall beat the French."[1] Lord Harrington, the
Secretary of State in whose department the most important part of the negotiation was officially conducted,
leaned strongly for war. The Opposition raised the
familiar cry for national honour and fidelity to our
allies. The emperor sent envoy after envoy to intrigue
for Walpole's overthrow. Fleury, with a council of
state full of marshals, had difficulties of his own, and he
more than once betrayed the British minister by shifts,
tricks, evasions, and downright lying. Walpole for
a long time stood entirely alone. He held out resolutely against armed intervention. "Madam," he
said complacently to the queen one morning (1734),
"there are fifty thousand men slain this year in Europe,

[1] Hervey, ii. 42.

and not one Englishman." He kept his hand firm on
the helm, scanning every shift of wind and current at
Vienna, Madrid, Versailles, the Hague, and making a
series of tacks so skilful and so effectual that even at
this distance of time it is impossible for a political
reader not to follow them with some of the lively
interest that is commonly reserved for our own
affairs.

He read all the despatches that arrived or were sent;
he carried on an unwearied private correspondence of
his own with his brother and other agents at the continental courts; and he personally directed the whole of
a long course of negotiations, as intricate and as delicate
as any European statesman ever meddled with. It is
important to remark that though Walpole was firmly
decided that not an Englishman should be killed either
to support Augustus in Poland, or to recover the Italian
possessions of the House of Austria, he was too much
alive to the immense difficulty of keeping England out
of the war if it should continue, not to strain every
nerve for the pacification of Europe. First, he contrived
gradually to secure from the court an unwilling acquies-
cence in his endeavours, before departing from our own
neutrality, to bring about a general peace. Nowhere
was caution more necessary. "Step by step," he said, " I
can carry the king and queen perhaps the road I wish,
but if I ever show them at a distance to what end that
road leads, they stop short." Second, he laboured in
the Cabinet, just as he was accustomed to do in
Parliament, by reasoning, persuasion, and steady command of the facts as they were, to convert his
colleagues. For, says his brother in a casual remark

of much significance in the controversy as to Walpole's arbitrary and dictatorial methods, "powerful as he was, he never would let his own opinion, in matters of State, prevail against the majority of them." [1]

The third and most exacting part of his task, besides holding back his own court and directing his own Cabinet, was to put such equal pressure now on the emperor, now on the cardinal, now on the court of Spain, as would force them to an adjustment. The emperor was bent on recovering his footing in Italy; the queen of Spain, on securing Naples for Don Carlos, and his duchies for his brothers; France coveted aggrandisement on her eastern frontier at the expense of the Empire. The emperor was stubborn, proud, and dull. Fleury was naturally disposed to peace, but his hand was forced by colleagues with designs on Germany, and he was not without the duplicity of weakness. The queen of Spain was a fury. The pensionary of the United Provinces was a martyr to the gout, was rough, peevish, and unmanageable; and the other Dutch leaders were all suspicious and distracted. Such were the personages with whom the British minister had to deal.

As usual, Walpole approached his difficulties step by step. The two maritime powers, Great Britain and Holland, held the key of the position. Any hope of assistance from them would harden the haughty and warlike temper of Vienna. On this side it was necessary to force into the mind of the emperor, that on no terms could he expect aid either from English or Dutch. On the other hand, the apprehension that the Dutch would

[1] Coxe's *Mem. of Horace Walpole*, i. 328.

act with vigour was the strongest of the reasons why
France should come to honourable terms. If the maritime powers should hold aloof, she would suppose herself to have the Empire at her mercy. It will be seen
how nice was the triple equipoise in which Walpole
had to keep his representations at Vienna one day, at
Versailles the next, and at the Hague every day.

After this exercise of delicate pressure on the emperor, a second leading object was to divide Spain from
France. Each was in constant alarm lest the other
should come to an accommodation with Vienna. Walpole caused France to be assured that if she did not
make peace, a marriage would be agreed upon between
an Austrian archduchess and one of the Spanish princes,
to the detriment and isolation of the interests of France.
Spain, on the other hand, was discreetly informed of the
existence of secret communications between Versailles
and Vienna. The scene is not particularly edifying to
those who hope that politics are a branch of morals.
Walpole's part, at any rate, was upright and consistent. He was no Machiavellian, engaged in a selfish
match of fraud and craft, but an honest statesman,
striving at once for the best interests both of his own
country and her neighbours. Instead of making England a party to a war in which she had not a shadow of
concern, he made her the umpire and pacificator of
Europe. In concert with Holland he submitted (1735)
a plan of accommodation at the three courts. The plan
contained no advantage to France, and so people laughed
at it. Bolingbroke, however, shrewdly observed that
Walpole was no fool, and there must be more in it than
yet appeared. So it proved, for Walpole had discovered

the design of France upon Lorraine, and that it might
be possible for the emperor to find compensation in
Tuscany. A new element of danger suddenly appeared
in a quarrel between Spain and Portugal, but Walpole
sent the British fleet to the Tagus as a hint of moderation to Portugal, and the mediation of England and
France once more repressed an outbreak. After some
months of further negotiation a general pacification was
arranged. The Spanish Bourbon was installed in Naples
and Sicily; the Saxon elector was recognised as King of
Poland; Tuscany, on the death of the reigning grand
duke, was to go to Francis of Lorraine, the destined
husband of Maria Theresa; Lorraine on this event
(which happened very conveniently in 1737) was to
belong to Stanislaus for life, and then to be ceded to
France. Our generation has seen the overthrow of this
settlement—has seen the Bourbons expelled from Naples
and Sicily, the Austrians from Tuscany, and the French
from Lorraine: we do not need to be told how much
future trouble to the world was involved in the various
arrangements of 1735-38. Walpole's defence for the
cession of Lorraine—that it was a province of which
France had taken and kept possession in every war in
which she had been engaged—was unsatisfactory, but it
may be counted a sufficiently good defence for the times.
To modern sentiment there is something deeply repugnant
in this insolent transfer of whole populations, with no
more regard to race, to tradition, or to their own wishes,
than if they were flocks and herds in a cattle-market.
The idea of a federal and independent Italy was not
altogether unknown. But to attempt to found a foreign
policy on nationality in the first half of the eighteenth

century, would have been generally deemed as impossible
and as much of an anachronism, as in the second half
of the nineteenth it would be to exclude or to ignore
nationality. No effort on the part of Great Britain
could have averted territorial re-arrangement: it was
something to effect it with the least possible confusion.

Walpole for once got perhaps even more credit than he
deserved. Carteret declared that he always thought
Walpole the luckiest dog that ever meddled with public
affairs. Pulteney said it was a most fortunate event for
England, and whoever had the honour of it, he was glad
England had the benefit of it. Bolingbroke put it that
if the English ministers had a hand in the peace, they
had more sense than he thought they had; and if they
had no hand in it, then they had much better luck than
they deserved.

We now come to the most critical affair in Walpole's
career. Having successfully steered through foreign
emergencies for so many years, in 1738 he encountered a
storm in his own country, which all his address and
persistency were powerless to quell, and which finally
brought his power to destruction. The origins of the
Spanish war of 1739 would furnish a long story. But
the character of that war is described in a single sentence.
It was, like the greater war of Pitt fifteen years later,
what Adam Smith calls a colony quarrel,[1] and its object
was to prevent the search of the colony ships carrying
on a contraband trade with the Spanish main. By the
Treaty of Utrecht a single British ship was allowed to
trade with Spanish America. The annual ship became
the colourable shelter of an extensive illicit trade; con-

---

[1] *Wealth of Nations*, bk. iv. ch. 7.

sorts followed her, and she was incessantly replenished with fresh supplies; while at the same time, under thin pretence of refitting and provisioning, other ships carried on smuggling operations wherever they could run a boat ashore. That all this was illegal, that Spain was warranted in search and capture, that occasionally these rights were harshly exercised in distant seas and under proconsuls too far off to be under control by the Government at Madrid, and that this harshness was often provoked by the daring of the English traders, are all facts which a few years after the war had broken out nobody could be found seriously to deny. Burke says that it was his fortune to converse with many of Walpole's enemies, who stirred up the clamour against Spain as successfully as Burke himself in after years stirred up the clamour against France. "None of them," he says, "no, not one, did in the least defend the measure, or attempt to justify their conduct, which they as freely condemned as they would have done in commenting on any proceeding in history in which they were totally unconcerned."[1]

For the moment no justification was necessary. The merchants set the nation on fire with the tale of atrocities on the Spanish main. Gentlemen read letters to the House of Commons about seventy of our brave sailors lying in chains in Spanish dungeons. "Our countrymen in chains!" cried a city alderman in his place in Parliament, "and slaves to Spaniards! Is not this enough to fire the coldest? And shall we sit here debating about words and forms while the sufferings of our countrymen call loudly for redress?" Sea-captains

---

[1] *Regicide Peace*, vol. viii. 147 (ed. 1818).

came to the bar of the House and told—not on oath, and without liability to cross-examination—how free-born Englishmen were loaded with irons, fed on the vilest food, overrun with vermin, and driven to work like galley-slaves for Spanish taskmasters. The famous Captain Jenkins was produced to inform Parliament how, seven years before, his ship had been boarded by a Spanish *guarda-costa*, and his ear had been brutally torn off, with the taunt that he had better carry it to his king. On being asked what he thought when he found himself in such ill plight, Jenkins replied, in a phrase which became the cry of the hour, "I commended my soul to my God and my cause to my country." The neat balance of the sentence has not the ring of the rough seafarer; but the literary prompter, whoever he may have been, knew his business. When the country suffers itself to be swept by such stories as these, it ceases to be rigorous as to evidence and proof; the possibility of exaggeration and invention made no difference in the effect. Recital of cruelty is the surest means of rousing the passionate indignation of Englishmen. They are not incapable of cruel deeds themselves, as some deplorable episodes in Ireland and the East and West Indies have shown. But to their honour it may be said that their sensibilities are readily touched; and when, as in the present case, to humanity was added both national pride and commercial ambition, then, in the alderman's phrase, it was indeed idle to talk about forms and words, even though forms and words chanced to mean policy, legality, and international right.

Walpole agreed with the rest of the public that the conduct of the Spanish governors and captains deserved

the sharpest resentment, but he believed that redress
for the past and security for the future could be obtained
by peaceable means. He knew that the fresh activity
of the guardships in Spanish America was connected
with Spanish objects in Europe, and he had satisfied
himself that these objects could be more surely handled
by diplomacy here than by buccaneers there. He insisted that war with the nation with whom our trade
was greatest, would do us more harm than anything to
be gained from it would do us good. He warned
Parliament that France would certainly join Spain, and
that, for various reasons, neither the emperor, nor
Holland, nor Sweden would assist us. By these arguments he gained time, and a preliminary convention
was made with Spain. Plenipotentiaries were to meet
at Madrid to regulate the future relations of the two
countries in respect of trade and navigation, and the
various other questions in dispute. With unmeasured
heat the Opposition denounced the convention, and re-
echoed the passionate cry of the nation for war. Walpole declared that war would be unjust, impolitic, and
dishonourable. He carried the House of Commons with
him by a slender majority of eight and twenty, but
public opinion went every day farther away from peace.
The pith of the English demand was abolition of the
right of search, and right of search was what Spain
would not concede, and after nine years of war still did
not concede. Appeal to national pride proved to be a
game at which two could play, and the insulting language of the Opposition roused in the people of Spain
anger as hot against British buccaneers as that of Englishmen against Spanish guardships. The plenipotentiaries

met in May (1739), but it was evident from the first that war was inevitable. The actual declaration was made in October, and was received in England with a frenzy of enthusiasm. "Ah! they are ringing the bells to-day," said Walpole, "they will soon be wringing their hands."

Then why did not Walpole resign? He had declared the war to be unjust, impolitic, and dishonourable; he had predicted disaster and confusion as its result; he was surrounded by colleagues who did not share his views, and who thwarted, embarrassed, and intrigued against him; neither court nor people went with him, and he was so conscious of the weakness of his position that he did actually and repeatedly press his resignation upon the king. Why did he not persist in it? That he was bound to refuse to have part or lot in a war which he believed, and had declared, to be unjust and dishonourable it is wholly impossible to deny. This was not the case of the excise over again. There the public rejected a boon which he had gratuitously devised for them and proposed to them; the country would be no worse off after its rejection than it was before; the boon might be proffered again on another day. But to lend himself to an unjust and unnecessary war, was worse than if he had deliberately aided and abetted the South Sea scheme after denouncing it as fraught with national disaster.

The case against Walpole is too clear to deserve argument, but we are curious for explanation. It is not always safe to suppose the lowest motives to be the truest, even in politics. Those who find the key to Walpole's character in his thirst for power at any price

and under all circumstances, have their explanation
ready-made. It is not a very plausible one, on the face
of it. If the retention of power had been his only
thought, it would, as he said, have been his interest that
there should be war;[1] he would have been safer if he
had flung himself, as Pitt, Pulteney, and the rest flung
themselves, headlong into the current of public passion.
But if Walpole was, as we hold, a sound statesman, with
clear vision and genuine public spirit, it is necessary to
seek some other account of what was not only, on his
own showing, connivance at a crime, but was a gross mis-
calculation. As Bolingbroke said, Walpole was no fool.
Considerations of real weight must have been present
in his mind. We must remember, to begin with, that
he had passed his whole life in surmounting difficulties,
and bringing bad situations to good ends. He had not
liked the Treaty of Hanover much better than he liked
the Spanish war, yet he had turned it to good account.
So with many other transactions in which he had been
engaged. "I never heard," he said about this time, in
a sentence which explains one great source of his strength,
"*I never heard that it is a crime to hope for the best.*" He
undoubtedly hoped that by remaining in office he would
there be best able to seize the first opportunity, or if
not the first, then the second or the third, of finding
for the war, mistaken as it was, a speedy and a safe
issue. His adversaries were fully alive to this. One of
their strongest charges against him was that he had no
intention of making war in good earnest, and that he
would cheat his own country by bringing the war to
an end without forcing Spain to acknowledge the

[1] Coxe, ch. 51, iv. 55.

right of British vessels freely to navigate the American
seas.

Then, again, Walpole must have known, as the event
so swiftly proved, that his opponents, as they then
stood, were incapable of forming a strong government,
of conducting a war with vigour or making a peace
with skill, and that not one of them was comparable to
himself in experience, knowledge, or ability, either as
negotiator or administrator. Pitt as yet was only a
declaimer, Carteret was a marvel of temerity and levity,
and Pulteney, as we shall presently see, had neither
nerve nor judgment for a crisis. Walpole might almost
be excused for asking himself whether it could be his
duty to leave the fate of his country to men who had
shown themselves so recklessly unscrupulous and unprincipled, and who were destined, as he foresaw, to
show themselves so profoundly incompetent. Finally,
he may, without any baseness, have felt some of that
special allegiance towards the king, which within limits
we regard as a virtue when shown towards friends and
colleagues in a party. The king's appeal, "Will you
desert me in my greatest difficulties?" was not one that
after so many years of service Walpole could listen to
with indifference. That he should have made himself
an accomplice in an unjust and mischievous foreign war
in order to help George II, was like Mr. Pitt's abandonment of the Catholic claim at the risk of a civil war to
please King George's grandson. None of these pleas,
however, stand good before the tribunal of history;
they may explain, but they cannot extenuate this grave
error in Walpole's career, or efface the one serious stain
on his political reputation.

The death of the emperor in 1740 was the signal for
an immense outbreak of perfidy and rapine. Powers
that had solemnly guaranteed the succession of his
daughter to the hereditary dominions of her house, one
after another poured troops into her provinces, and set
about the dismemberment of Austria. Walpole urged a
pacification between Maria Theresa and Frederick of
Prussia, as the first step towards a union of Germany
against the designs of France. But his counsels no
longer commanded attention either at home or abroad,
and in the great changes wrought by Frederick on the
European stage, he did not survive to play a part.
When Walpole fell, as Ranke truly says, "it was not the
fall of an ordinary minister, but the fall of the political
system based upon the first union of the house of Hanover with the Regent of France. It was a return to the
policy then abandoned of war against France and the
Bourbon interest in Europe, and that at a moment when
these once more had the upper hand both by land and
sea."[1] He had brought the parliamentary constitution
safely through its perils, though it was destined to new
perils at a later epoch from the vigorous and obstinate
reaction under George III; and the close of the constitutional movement at home left the way open for Pitt to
conduct new enterprises abroad.

[1] Ranke's *History of England*, v. 405.

CHAPTER XI

WALPOLE'S FALL

THOSE who can recall the state of public feeling towards the coalition Government of Lord Aberdeen at the time of the Crimean War, will be able to realise the impatience and exasperation provoked by Walpole towards 1740. The general sentiment could not then organise and express itself with the extraordinary velocity and concentrated force—a velocity and a force not without peril of their own—to which we are so accustomed in the present day. But the great career which was opened by the genius and character of Pitt a few years later, demonstrated that even then it was possible for the tide of popular passion and enthusiasm to shake and to vanquish both court and Parliament. Walpole had placed himself in a completely false position, in which he could neither guide nor check, neither satisfy nor resist the judgment, prepossessions, passions of the dominant orders and interests of the country. The national pride and temper were thoroughly roused. People had become profoundly fatigued with twenty years of good sense; it seems as if nothing were so hard for a nation to sustain as a long course of mere prudence. That spirit which its admirers call enterprise, adventure, and energy, and

which those who do not admire it, call cupidity in disguise, had become irresistible.   It has been very truly
remarked that the English bring to the government of
their mercantile interests the same stiffness and pride as
Louis XIV brought to his dynastic interests.   The war
with Spain was a war for trade, for exclusive markets,
for the mines of Peru and Potosi.   It was a war for
plunder.   With such a mood in full blast, Walpole could
not grapple.   Burke put his finger upon the fatal spot
when he said that Walpole, while professing to share the
sentiments of his adversaries, opposed their practical in-
ferences, and that this for a political commander is the
choice of a weak post.[1]   No observation could be more
true, and the more popular the system of government, the
truer is the application.   To temporise, to manage, to find
intermediate positions, to play a fine game, is in popular
governments unintelligible and impracticable.   The
England of the Hanoverian kings was popular enough
for this maxim to apply with all its force in moments
of agitation, as Walpole found out.

The Duke of Newcastle saw his chance, and to Walpole's other embarrassments was now added personal
dissension in the Cabinet.   The duke flung himself
eagerly into the designs of the war party.   Lord Hardwicke, the Chancellor, always took sides with the duke.
Wilmington, who had never forgotten his own miserable
failure in 1727, thought that the opportunity of being
first minister was again returning to him, as indeed it
was.   There were, in short, not more than three members of the Cabinet on whom Walpole could securely
count.   The king was frequently irritated at the min-

[1] *First Letter on Regicide Peace*, viii. 147.

ister's refusal to come into his policy, but the staunchness of his character stood the test. "I do not care for the Opposition," he told Newcastle, "if all my servants act together; but if they thwart one another, then indeed it will be another case." The royal remonstrances could not abate the duke's peevishness and restlessness. Violent altercations took place every day. "I oppose nothing," said Walpole on one of these occasions, "I give in to everything, am said to do everything, am to answer for everything, and yet, God knows, I dare not do what I think right. I am of opinion for leaving more ships of Sir Challoner Ogle's squadron behind, but I dare not, and I will not make any alteration." The archbishop pacifically proposed postponement of the question, but Walpole refused. "Let them go," he cried, "let them go." A struggle took place on a vacancy in the Cabinet. In 1740 Walpole wished to make Lord Hervey Privy Seal. The duke, to prevent the appointment, asked Carteret whether he would take it. In the Cabinet he suggested that it should be offered to Carteret. Walpole said he was not sure that it would be accepted. The duke replied that he would answer for that. "Oh," cried Walpole, "I always suspected that you had been dabbling there, and now I know it. But if you make such bargains, I don't think myself obliged to keep them." Hervey had the office, and within a few months, when Walpole's hour of danger came, Hervey turned his back upon him.[1] In his memoirs he has described a scene between the two ministers at the end of a long meeting of the Cabinet, which deserves to be transcribed—

[1] H. W. to Mann, 7th January 1741, i. 112.

" Just as Sir Robert Walpole was upon his legs to go away, the Duke of Newcastle said, 'If you please, I would speak one word to you before you go'; to which Sir Robert Walpole replied, 'I do not please, my lord; but if you will, you must.'—'Sir, I shall not trouble you long.'—'Well, my lord, that's something; but I had rather not be troubled at all. Won't it keep cold till to-morrow?'—'Perhaps not, sir.'— 'Well, come then, let's have it'; upon which they retired to a corner of the room, where his Grace whispered very softly, and Sir Robert answered nothing but aloud, and said nothing aloud but every now and then, 'Pooh! Pshaw! O Lord! O Lord! pray be quiet. My God, can't you see it is over?'"[1]

The leaders of the Opposition had in 1739 taken the unwise step of seceding from the House, as an expression of their disgust at the ruin which the minister was bringing on the country. The House of Commons is the worst place in the world for *coups-de-théâtre*. Their secession, like that of Fox and his friends, was a great mistake, and when they perceived the difficulties that were thickening round their redoubtable opponent they hurried back. The Parliament had now approached its last session, and both sides had their attention fixed on the general election. It was with a view of bringing on the topics of their whole case against the minister, that the Opposition in the beginning of 1741 introduced in both Houses of Parliament their famous motion, that an humble address be presented to his Majesty that he would be graciously pleased to remove the Right Honourable Sir Robert Walpole, knight of the most noble order of the Garter, First Commissioner, Chancellor and Under-Treasurer of the Exchequer, and one of his Majesty's most honourable Privy Council, from his Majesty's presence and counsels for ever. The

[1] *Memoirs*, iii. 370, 371.

debate in the Commons (13th February 1741) began at one
o'clock in the afternoon in a crowded House. The passages were thronged, and some members had even come
down so early as six in the winter morning to secure
their seats. Sandys opened the assault, and on the
same day Carteret made the same motion in the House
of Lords. Their topics were common. In foreign
affairs the great article of charge was that the minister
had abandoned our old and natural ally, the House of
Austria, and raised up our inveterate enemy, the House
of Bourbon. In domestic affairs he had fraudulently
mismanaged the South Sea settlement, had failed to
reduce the national debt, and had swollen the expenditure on Spithead expeditions and Hyde Park reviews,
while his unconstitutional conduct had been seen in a
standing army of unnecessary numbers, costly and useless squadrons, parliamentary corruption, the erection of
new and useless offices, a swollen civil list, heavy taxation, and the dismissal of officers for voting against the
excise scheme. These acts of profligate impolicy and
maladministration were due to one who had arrogated to
himself a place of French extraction, that of sole minister,[1]
contrary to the nature and principles of the English
constitution. Even, however, if no oversight, error, or
crime were supposed in his public conduct, still in a free
government "too long possession of power is dangerous."
It was not necessary to prove him guilty of specific
crimes ; as things stood, the mere dissatisfaction of
the people and their suspicion of his conduct were

---

[1] Richelieu first assumed the quality of prime minister, and it
was for long as odious in France as it became a century later in
England. See *Œuvres du Card. de Retz*, i. 281 (ed. 1870).

sufficient causes for his removal from the counsels of the king.

The motion had no sooner been made than it was proposed that Walpole should withdraw, on the strength of a well-known practice of the House, that a member against whom an accusation has been brought should retire while his conduct is being inquired into. Both this, however, and the hardly less absurd amendment that he should be heard in his own defence and then withdraw, were dismissed. After a long and vehement discussion, in which Pulteney and Pitt were most conspicuous in the attack, Walpole wound up the debate in a speech which, so far as we can judge from the condensed report, was marked by an animation, comprehensiveness, and dignity worthy of a great minister defending a long and powerful government of the affairs of a great nation.[1]

He vindicated his foreign policy and his financial administration; taunted his enemies for reproaching government with pusillanimity if they did not interfere in foreign affairs, and with Quixotism if they did; asked how he could answer charges that were not specific, and were substantiated by nothing more tangible than common fame and public notoriety; insisted that if he had governed by means of corrupt and profligate expenditure, then King, Lords, and Commons for twenty years must all have been his dupes or accomplices, which was surely proving too much; declared that the war had from the beginning been carried on with as much vigour as was consistent with our safety and our circumstances

---

[1] The minutes of the speech are given by Coxe, ch. 56, vol. iv. p. 184.

when the war broke out; and, finally, came to an end
with a warm denial of charges of gratifying personal
ambition, usurping sole authority, grasping at emoluments or grants for himself, or placing those connected
with him in posts of responsibility or trust for which
they were unfit.

It is no esoteric secret confined to the precincts of
Parliament, that a taunt, or a personality, or an appeal
to any peculiar combination of parties, often goes further for purposes of debate than either lofty declamation
or weighty reasoning. Walpole opened his speech with
what was the most apt and vital part of it, a vigorous
assault upon the composition of the assailing body. The
Jacobites, he said, distress the government they would
fain subvert; the Tories contend for party prevalence
and power; the Patriots, impatient for office, clamour
for change of measures, but mean only change of ministers. "A patriot, sir! why, patriots spring up like
mushrooms! I could raise fifty of them within the four
and twenty hours. I have raised many of them in one
night. It is but refusing to gratify an unreasonable or
an insolent demand, and up starts a patriot."

The coalition which Walpole denounced, did not hold
together until the division. The movement had been
ill concerted. It was devised by some of the malcontent
Whigs, without consulting the Tories. Not even all
the Prince of Wales's men voted. The most surprising
event of the debate was the declaration of Shippen that
he regarded the motion as only a scheme for turning out
one minister and bringing in another; that it was quite
indifferent to him who was in and who was out; and
that he would give himself no concern in the question.

When the time came, he and thirty-four of his friends walked out. Bolingbroke lost all patience with virtue so maladroit. The conduct of the Tories, he said, is silly, infamous, and void of any colour of excuse. It was certainly hard to reconcile with their general conduct on other occasions.

The motion was thrown out by 290 against 106 in the Commons, and 108 against 59 in the Lords. It was noticed that 500 members were present at the height of the debate, so that more than a hundred must have gone away without voting. The majority was crushing so far as it went, but the Opposition had been able to state their view of the issue before the constituencies and their owners. As a Jacobite well said, *it marked Walpole out to the nation.* The advantage of concentrating attention on a single personality, whether that attention be friendly or hostile, is a cardinal maxim among the mysteries of electioneering. That Walpole felt himself and his policy in deeper and more perilous waters than he had ever to face before, is certain. This was the time when his son drew that melancholy picture of him, almost the only melancholy one there is—

" He who was asleep as soon as his head touched the pillow, for I have frequently known him snore ere they had drawn his curtains, now never sleeps above an hour without waking ; and he, who at dinner always forgot he was minister, and was more gay and thoughtless than all his company, now sits without speaking, and with his eyes fixed for an hour together."

It has even been contended. incredible as it may seem, that Walpole himself, the most powerful defender of the Revolution, at this time made overtures to the Pretender.

It will be allowed that very strong proof is needed to confirm a story so opposed to all the rational probabilities of the case; but the mystery ought not to be passed over, and Lord Stanhope is surely in the right when he censures Coxe for omitting all mention of the document from which the mystery arises, though Coxe must have had it in his hands. The story is this. Among Walpole's papers was found a letter from James, dated from Rome in July 1739, and endorsed in Walpole's own writing as being an original letter, as having been addressed and given in Rome to Carte, the Jacobite historian, and as afterwards delivered to himself by Carte in September. The letter is a reply from James to some message transmitted to him by Carte from an important person in England, to the effect that this person wished well to James and his cause, and had it in his power to serve both. The message would seem to have asked for the old assurances that the King, if restored to the throne, would protect the Church of England and inflict no vengeance on the Hanoverian princes. These assurances James was, of course, perfectly ready to give, but he evidently distrusted the authenticity of the message. "The message you bring," he says to Carte, "could not but appear very singular and extraordinary to me, because *you deliver it only from second-hand*, and that I have *no proof of your being authorised by the person in question*, who cannot but feel that it is natural for me to mistrust what may come from him."[1] Carte, we must remember, though a strong and an honest Jacobite, was not a regular political agent by profession; he was a student, and was at this time immersed in research for the pur-

---

[1] Stanhope's *Hist. of Eng.*, iii. Appendix, 50, 51.

poses of his history of England.   Part of that research
he was at the moment industriously prosecuting in the
royal archives in Paris, and no doubt he made frequent
journeys between the two capitals.   But James evidently
felt it impossible to believe that a man of this stamp
was likely to be chosen by Walpole as the bearer of so
delicate and dangerous a communication.

If the letter had not borne Walpole's own endorse-
ment, nobody would believe that it was he to whom
James referred.   Everybody would then have taken it
for granted that it was an intercepted letter, and that
the reference was to one of the malcontent Whigs in
opposition.   As it is, two important facts are to be observed.   The author of the message, whoever he was,
did not communicate his good wishes towards the Pretender direct to Carte, but to some third person.   We
are asked to assume, therefore, that Walpole, one of the
wiliest of men, actually told somebody else to tell Carte
that he wished well to the Pretender, and had his interest
at heart.   Next, Carte was unable to satisfy James that
he had any authority to bring the message at all.
In other words, these views, so absolutely irrecon-
cilable with every act and utterance of his life, so profoundly important, so extremely dangerous, must have
been thrown out by Walpole fortuitously, gratuitously,
aimlessly, and without authority to anybody to convey
them to the only man from whom he could expect any return for these momentous confidences.   The only document
that we have, therefore, cannot reasonably be taken as
good evidence for so startling a statement as that Walpole
made overtures to the Pretender, either insincerely, with
a hope of winning James's support at the general elec-

tion (which was more than two years off at the time
of these overtures), or for any other purpose whatever.

Two hypotheses occur to us. The one is that Walpole had nothing at all to do with the message; that the
sender of it was somebody else in his camp; and that
Carte gave Walpole James's letter to convince him that
grave designs were afoot, and that it was time for the
minister to recognise Jacobite power and influence. The
other explanation is that in conversation with Carte's in-
formant, Walpole may have in general terms admitted
the possibility, in the event of a war and all the difficulties and complications of war, of a strong reaction
setting in against the House of Hanover; he may further
have intimated the apprehension, which for that matter
had never for twenty years been absent from his mind, and
was the basis of his whole policy, that if the Pretender
would make declarations in favour of the Church and
against vindictive retaliation, he might have a chance
of restoration to the throne of his ancestors. This was
mere matter of opinion on the facts. The Jacobite
plotter was the most credulous being in existence, and it
is easy to conceive that language of this kind, filtered
through several channels, may have emboldened Carte
to give James a message, in whose significance even the
Pretender himself, as his words show, did not for a
moment believe. This is the explanation of the mysterious paper, which seems to us to have fewest difficulties.
No explanation can have so many as that which assumes
that Walpole entered into a dangerous intrigue for the
bare chance of two or three votes. This is the most
incredible of all, not merely because the intrigue would

have been disgraceful, but because he must have known
that it would be hopelessly futile.

The general election took place at midsummer (1741).
The Duke of Argyll exerted all his influence against
Walpole in Scotland, where the affair of Captain Porteous
had not been forgiven. Then, as now, Scotland was
almost unanimous, and only six out of the forty-five
members were for the court. The forty-two boroughs of
Cornwall, under Lord Falmouth and other patrons,
proved almost as unfavourable. The Cornish Tories had
made a vigorous attack in the election of 1734, but had
failed ignominiously. They succeeded in 1741, partly
because the Falmouth influence had gone over to them,
and partly because the Prince of Wales now actively
intervened, and his power, as Duke of Cornwall, of
asserting dormant or disputable rights, was too dangerous to be left out of account by these small corporations.
When the time came, it was the Scottish vote and the
Cornish vote that destroyed the minister. Walpole's
attempt to divide the coalition between the malcontent
Whigs, the Tories, and the Jacobites, which had been
successful in the House, failed in the country ; and the
world beheld the curious sight of all the influence of the
Pretender being thrown into the same scale with all the
influence of the heir to the throne.

When the new Parliament met, Walpole's friends
were sanguine enough to look for a majority of forty,
and they calculated that a good majority, like a good
sum of money, tends to make itself bigger. In our time
we should know to a man, on the morrow of a general
election, how the newly-chosen members would go, and
whether they were for or against the Government of the

day. In the time of patrons and boroughmongers the caprice, the ambition, the selfishness of the individual had wider scope, and made calculation impossible. Not a day was lost before the two hosts eagerly joined battle. On the address Pulteney made a grand attack, to which Walpole replied, as his party thought, with as much health, spirits, force, and command as ever. He showed that he meant to fight every inch. He flung aside the charge that he was answerable for all the public troubles. Was it he who had raised war in Germany, or advised war with Spain, or killed either the Emperor Charles or the King of Prussia, or been the adviser of Frederick or of the King of Poland, or kindled the war between Muscovy and Sweden? He had brought about not one of these critical events; but if they meant to turn him out, the sooner he knew it the better; and if any man would move for a day to examine the state of the nation, he would second it. Chesterfield, he said, was right in telling the Lords that this was a time for truth, for plain truth, for English truth.

The unresting sea itself is less inconstant than are the moods of the House of Commons. After their chief's defiant speech, ministerialists had flocked home to their suppers in brilliant spirits; but when the serious work of deciding election petitions began on the following afternoon, they were promptly awakened to the dangers in front of them. Disputed returns were then decided, not as now by a judicial tribunal, nor as in an interval between then and now by select committees, but by the whole House, and without a pretence of judicial impartiality. The petitions were settled by purely political considerations. The engagement opened with a division on one of the Cornish petitions. The minister won, but he won only by seven out of four hundred and thirty-seven. The alternative of Downing Street or the Tower was thus seen to be a startling possibility. The next trial of strength was the election of the chairman of committees. Excitement was raised to the keenest pitch, for there was an uncertain band whose votes would depend on their instinct for a majority, or who, if they could not trust their instinct, would abstain. In either case the issue was doubtful. Two great party dinners were held at two taverns, and after dining at six o'clock, the House met in that tumult of hope, fear, expectancy, confidence, indecision which on such high occasions quickens the pulse of the dullest and the coolest. The lobbies were crowded, for four hundred and eighty members out of a gross total of five hundred and fifty-eight voted.

The tellers at last, amid breathless suspense, announced the numbers. Walpole's nominee was beaten by a majority of four. Pulteney and his men raised a great shout, loud, fierce, and long, — the exultant rebound after twenty years of unbroken defeat. For twenty years they had been fortified by the accession of one man of genius after another; for twenty years they had exhausted the resources of wit, passion, and power in debate; they had practised every manœuvre in the art of parliamentary tactics; they had divided only once in a session, and they had harassed the foe with divisions; they had taunted him with parsimony, and reviled him for profusion; they had held him up to contempt for clinging to peace, and to execration for running the risk of war; they had scourged him in public prints, and stealthily sapped him at court; and yet after twenty years of ingenious and relentless effort, only a few months before this night they had been so baffled that they had actually marched away in the sullenness of defeat and despair, leaving their adversary smiling, composed, unhurt, the master of the field. And now at last the spell was broken. They suddenly held their enemy at bay. They had no right to the stern joy of victors in a great public cause, but we cannot wonder that their exultation was the most boisterous that had ever been heard within the walls of Saint Stephen's Chapel, or that some of the wilder among them even reminded one another that *forty-one* was a date of ill omen for tyrant ministers,—it was just a hundred years since patriots had brought the guilty Strafford to the block.

The division lists began to fluctuate. For a few days after the first defeat, the minister had small majorities. Government won by seven, by twenty-four, by twenty-one, then they lost by four, by one,—so nice was the balance. On the important question of the Westminster petition, their men were thrown out by a majority again of four. There was no baseness to which men did not stoop. A young Irish peer was brought in for Winchilsea by the court. His competitor, though he had only a single vote at the election, presented a petition. The sitting member made a heroic speech, then went across to the Opposition, and promised if they would withdraw the Winchilsea petition, he would support them on the case of Westminster. This single vote lost Walpole one of the questions connected with that decisive event. Every point was fought, and the sittings were longer than ever were known. His opponents sank so low in their exasperation as to bethink themselves of Saturday sittings, as an ingenious means of depriving him of the air and exercise without which he could not live. Sir Robert held to his post, and made speeches at four o'clock in the morning as strong and as full of spirit as his speeches had ever been. His sons hoped that as soon as he had gained success enough for honour, and made the majority secure, he would be induced to quit the scene and end his career with some years of repose. But the veteran only laughed over the supper-table, and declared that he was younger than any of them.

The Christmas holidays arrived before the struggle was over, and were busily spent in urging the consciences and interests of wavering members. Spirit ran so high both indoors and outside, that not even the neediest member dared to offer his vote in return for a place, a pension, or cash down. There were over forty of them on whom neither side could count. Some of them gave first a vote for Opposition, then a vote for ministers, and the third time no vote at all; and then the order of their conscientious rotation began afresh. Horace Walpole had not long been back from Rome, where they had been electing a pope ; the intrigues among members of Parliament reminded him of nothing so much as the dealings of the cardinals in the sacred conclave. Such was the desperate tenacity of the minister, that he actually wrung from the king permission to send an envoy informally to offer the Prince of Wales to raise his annual allowance from fifty to one hundred thousand pounds, to pay his debts, and to abandon all resentment and displeasure against him. The Prince replied, as Walpole might have been certain that he would reply, that he would listen to no such intimations, and that he desired to have no more of them until the retirement from power of the minister by whom he conceived himself to have been so deeply affronted and injured.

At the end of the recess, Pulteney instantly returned to the charge with a motion for a secret committee of twenty-one to inquire into the state of affairs, to send for persons and papers, and to give the king their advice. The thunder rattled from every oratorical battery. Great speeches were made on both sides, including, besides Walpole and Pulteney, Pitt, Henry Fox, George Grenville, and Yonge. Yonge was the minister of whom Walpole said that nothing but such a character could keep down such parts, and nothing but such parts support such a character. When the debate was over Pulteney, who, as has been said, always sat on the Treasury bench, cried in admiration to Sir Robert, "Well, nobody can do what you can." "Yes," replied Walpole, "Yonge did better." "No," Pulteney answered, "it was fine, but not of that weight with what you said." The whip had been vigorous. With the ardour that in a parliamentary crisis knows no bounds, they had dragged men from sick beds, and brought up lame, halt, and blind. The minister's eldest son, as auditor of the exchequer, had a residence that communicated with the House of Commons. He was sheltering two or three invalids there, until the question should be put. The patriots stuffed up the keyhole with dirt and sand, and the door could not be opened in time for the division. When the division was taken the members who voted made up 503, the greatest number that had ever been in the House, and the minister's majority in what would now be obviously treated as a strict vote of confidence, fell to three. It was evident that he was doomed.

Immediately after the overthrow of Pulteney's proposal for a secret committee, the case of the Chippenham petition was brought forward. On the previous question the friends of the minister lost by one, and on a later division on the merits by sixteen. While the last division was being taken, Walpole, who knew what was going to happen, beckoned one of the members whose seat was concerned, to come over and sit on the bench by his side. " Young man," he said, " I will tell you the history of all your friends as they come in, one by one. Such an one, I saved his brother from being hanged ; such another, from starving ; such another, I advanced both his sons." It was not in Walpole's nature to take reverses at a tragic pitch—that fatal defect in political affairs. He was free from all the cheap irony with which overstrained idealists find consolation for their own misreadings of human nature ; and the experience that " we men are but a little breed," neither soured nor embittered him. No statesman in history, not even Cavour after the crash of Villafranca, ever faced defeat more as a man should. This was the moment when Lord Morton wrote to Forbes : " Last week there passed a scene between Sir Robert and me by ourselves, that affected me more than anything I ever met with in my life. He has been sore hurt by flatterers, but has a great and an undaunted spirit, and a tranquillity something more than human." [1] Potter, the Archbishop of Canter-

[1] *Culloden Papers*, 175, 11th February 1742. See also 5th January 1741-42.

bury, one night at this time told Walpole that he had
been lately reading De Thou (an edition of De Thou had
just been published in England in seven stout folios),
and that he found a minister mentioned by him who,
having been long persecuted by his foes, at last van-
quished them, and the reason was *quia se non deseruit.*
Walpole was as good as the man in Thuanus. His
nerve never gave way, but as he informed the Duke of
Devonshire, then in Ireland, " the panic was so great
among what I should call my own friends, that they
all declared my retiring was become absolutely necessary,
as the only means to carry on the public business."

Between the two divisions on the Chippenham
petition, Walpole had made up his mind that all must
be over. Subterranean communications were carried on
with some of the old Whig leaders, and stipulations were
made that Walpole should be screened from all extreme
proceedings. The younger Whigs, with Pitt at their
head, strove to make their own peace with the court by
promising more liberal securities for the minister than
Pulteney was ready to do. They even undertook to
answer for the Prince of Wales. Walpole always rated
these aspirants at what was then their true political
value, and declined the offer. That the offer should
have been made, and on its rejection should have been
followed by unmeasured onslaughts on the minister
whom they had proposed to screen, is a good test of the
sincerity of all their heroic censures. When the arrangements with Pulteney were at last got into a fair train,
Walpole sought an audience at St. James's. The king,
who had so bravely supported him against the violence
of foes and the perfidy of friends, was deeply moved;

he fell on the minister's neck, wept, and kissed him,
and begged to see him frequently.[1] Private intimation
was sent to the Prince of Wales, and on the evening of
February 2, 1742, when the final division against him took
place, Walpole walked away for the last time out of that
famous chamber, where for forty years he had laboured
so assiduously for the national good, which had witnessed
so many of his triumphs, which had been the scene of so
long and undaunted a struggle against the most formidable enemies, and for which finally he had acquired new
prerogatives and an immovable supremacy in the constitution of the kingdom.

The conflict began on the first of December in 1741.
The House adjourned on the third of February, and on
the ninth Walpole was created Earl of Orford. Besides
this elevation it was arranged that he should receive a
pension of four thousand pounds a year ; the pension fell
through until 1744, when Walpole was driven by his
embarrassed circumstances to ask Pelham to obtain it for
him—a reasonable favour which that plausible personage,
who owed all to Walpole, granted with the worst possible
grace. The minister's first wife had died in 1737.
Then he married Mary Skerritt, with whom he had
lived for several years, and who only enjoyed her new
station for a few months. The child of this irregular
union was now, as part of the royal recognition of her
father's services, raised to the rank of an earl's daughter,
and kissed hands, amid some gibes, as Lady Mary
Walpole.

The drama did not end with Walpole's resignation.
Scenes of almost unparalleled confusion rapidly ensued.

[1] H. W. to Mann, 4th February.

The victorious coalition fell to pieces in the very hour of its triumph. Wyndham, who was justly described as the centre of union of the best men of all parties, had died on the eve of success (1740). They had no policy prepared, their tactics were not settled, and Pulteney, their leader, suddenly showed himself to be hopelessly bewildered and impotent. The country had taken the declamations of faction for the language of sincere belief and honest intention, and the popular expectations were boundless as they were distracted. There was a great cry for justice on the minister, and people were indignant at the criminal's audacity in daring to drive openly in the public streets. Others declared that they were not for blood, but that what the nation wanted was a good place bill, a pension bill, and triennial Parliaments. Some were for the reduction of the civil list, for life appointments, for abolishing regular troops. Others conceived the happily combined idea of doing away with all taxes, and carrying on the war with more vigour than ever. This wild babel of 1742 was the first example of the nemesis that awaits an Opposition that has been profligate in its promises. The bitterness of the disappointment was all in favour of the Jacobites, because it made people despair of any redress of their grievances from Parliament, and turned their minds towards a restoration. We are familiar with this particular effect of unreasonable expectations in France in our own day. This was always the Walpolean issue: a parliamentary commonwealth, or a legitimist restoration.

The one man who had a practical policy was the fallen minister, and his policy was the prosaic but very important one of keeping the Whig party together and continuing

the government in Whig hands. That was what Burke
meant by saying that Walpole's whole theory of government was by the instrument of party connection. That
was, and is, the secret of rule by Parliament. Walpole
had quitted Downing Street, but it was his influence and
address that still directed the contest. Pulteney, to whom
all looked as the head of the new government, on some
scruple that he had once declared that he would never
take emolument or office, accepted a seat in the Cabinet
but declined a department. No statesman has ever
made such an exhibition of infirmity as that of Pulteney
in 1742. He told Lord Shelburne some years afterwards
that there was no comprehending or describing the
confusion that prevailed ; that he lost his head, and was
obliged to go out of town for three or four days to keep
his senses.[1] Yet it was not courage in the ordinary meaning that failed him. It was rather, as a contemporary
observer said, a sense of shame that made him hesitate
at turning courtier, after having acted patriot so long
and with so much applause. He was shackled, moreover, by the stipulations into which he had entered
before Walpole's retirement; the feeling among his followers and in the country was too strong for him to let
them be known, or to appear to act on them ; and it may
be that he had no alternative but to stand in the back-
ground until the first fierceness of the storm had passed.
When that had gone, he found that his own chance was
ruined, and he was never able to retrieve it. Though
his action in this *gran rifiuto* was inexpressibly weak,
his judgment was clear. His view was that the trunk
of the government tree should be Whig, but a few

---

[1] *Life of Shelburne,* i. 47.

Tories might be grafted on it. The Tories, he told the
king, knew neither arithmetic nor foreign languages, and
therefore could not expect the first situations. The
Tories themselves thought differently. They had quite
enough arithmetic for quarter-day. They were all for a
clean sweep, the obliteration of old parties, and government on a Broad Bottom, in which they should have
their share. Bolingbroke hurried over from his medita-
tions on the sweets of retirement and the blessings of exile,
to share the day of glory with the men whose plans he
had inspired. The clever plotter found that it was he
who had been duped. The malcontent Whigs had no
intention of dividing the spoil. The result of this
discrepancy was in a few weeks a complete split between
the two main sections of the old Opposition, the extinc-
tion of Pulteney in a peerage, and the maintenance of all
Walpole's principal colleagues in office. Lord Wilmington
was in name the head of the government, Newcastle,
Hardwicke, Pelham, Yonge, all remained, and the only
change of real importance was the admission of Carteret
to be Secretary of State with the direction of foreign
affairs.

The next question after the division of places was
the punishment of the minister. There was much wild
talk of impeachment, and articles were even prepared.
But very little reflection showed that no crimes had yet
been brought home to the impenitent criminal, and that
there was nothing firmer to stand on than the hollow topics
of parliamentary invective. Then they fell back upon a
bill of pains and penalties, until they remembered that
though such a bill might pass the House of Commons, it
would certainly be thrown out by the Lords, and might

not even receive the assent of the king. Walpole had no doubt done what he could to make certain of his own security from the old-fashioned vengeance on fallen ministers. All ended in the appointment of a secret committee of the House of Commons to examine into the last ten years of Walpole's administration. This body was finally composed of twenty-one members, only two of whom were friendly to the incriminated man. They set to work with all the zeal of party and personal hatred, summoned agents, and ransacked papers. The papers disclosed nothing. Scrope, secretary of the Treasury, who knew more Treasury secrets than anybody else, would tell them nothing. He said he was fourscore years old, and did not care whether the last few months he had to live were spent in the Tower or not; the last thing he would do should be to betray the king, and next to him the Earl of Orford.

Walpole meanwhile only laughed at the secret committee. He laughed at a truly iniquitous bill which was brought in to aid the baffled committee, by giving an indemnity to anybody who would make discoveries as to the disposition of offices, or any payment or agreement in respect thereof, or concerning other matters belonging to the conduct of Robert Earl of Orford. The Lords threw out this odious project. Of the proceedings of the secret committee enough has been said on a previous page (122). As a grand exposure of the fallen minister, it was generally felt to have proved a complete failure. The mob had for a time daily carried his effigy in procession to the Tower. Horace Walpole one day ran up to one of these mobs to see what was the matter, and found a silly female figure, attended by three mock footmen,

and labelled "Lady Mary." The popular fury and contempt soon died away. When Pulteney by a ruinous
error of judgment allowed himself to be made Earl of
Bath, public wrath found a new channel. Walpole's
friends kept faith in a star which had been so long in
the ascendant. His house was more crowded than it
had ever been. One night in the summer (1742) his
son took him to Ranelagh. "It was pretty full," says
Horace, "and all its fulness flocked round us; we
walked with a train at our heels like two chairmen
going to fight, but they were extremely civil and did not
crowd him or say the least impertinence." When he
went to the levée, his former master could not conceal his
delight at seeing again the friend and author of so many
good counsels, and the new ministers were in an agony
lest the king should call him into the closet. They all,
however, kept that fair countenance which often among
political men hides such dismal emotions. They came
and spoke to him, and he had a long and jovial talk with
Chesterfield. Nobody seemed to bear anybody else malice.
The Duke of Newcastle gave his colleagues a dinner one
Sunday at Claremont; the servants got drunk and the
coachman tumbled off the box on the way back. They
were not far from Richmond, and the innkeeper told
them that perhaps Lord Orford would lend them his
coachman. So Walpole's coachman drove Pulteney, Carteret, and Limerick home. Carteret at a levée came up
to thank him, the Duke of Newcastle standing by.
"Oh, my lord," said Walpole, "whenever the duke is
near overturning you, you have nothing to do but to
send for me, and I'll save you."

Within a year of his fall the tide had begun to turn.

The public had found out the imposture. They drank
Sir Robert's health in all the clubs in the city, were for
making him a duke, and straightway putting him back
at the Treasury. They saw all in distraction : no union in
the court; no certainty about the House of Commons;
Lord Carteret making no friends, the king making
enemies, Mr. Pelham in vain courting Pitt, Pulteney
unresolved.[1] The common story that Walpole now
retired to his plantations and his pictures in Norfolk,
conveys a false impression. He was in fact only a
degree less important and less closely attentive to every
turn of affairs, both at home and abroad, than if he
had still been in office. Pelham and others of his colleagues went to visit him, and constantly corresponded
with him. Wilmington died in 1743, and after a
struggle with Carteret, Pelham, acting at every step
under the direct advice of Walpole, secured the first
post in the government. His mentor from Houghton,
adhering to his own cardinal maxim, warned him in
characteristic language to confine his colleagues to
one party,—"Whig it with all opponents that will
parley, but 'ware Tory." Nor can we doubt that the
other maxim present to Walpole was that the head of
the government should have commanding influence in
the House of Commons, and be a member of it. Pelham's administration lasted until his death in 1754. It
narrowly escaped shipwreck almost before it left port.
Carteret, thinking himself the ablest man in the Cabinet,
tried to carry all with a high hand, treated the rest as
ciphers, and trusted to his favour with the king to bring
him through. Give any man the crown on his side,

[1] H. W. to Mann, 12th October 1743, i. 275.

Carteret used to say, and he can defy everything.
Walpole's fall might have taught him how shallow was
his maxim. He is never sober, says Horace Walpole,
his rants are amazing; so are his parts and spirits. His
colleagues fled to Walpole for shelter and counsel. By
the beginning of 1744 the house in Arlington Street had
again become the centre of affairs. Carteret and Pelham
were his neighbours, and from their windows watched
the bustle at his door. "I know you all go to Lord
Orford," Carteret said, "he has more company than
any of us—do you think I can't go too?" As we shall
see, he did go. The struggle between Carteret and
the Pelhams was in one respect a counterpart of that
which went on for the first twenty-three years of the
reign of George III, and marked the strenuous effort
of the king to break the dominion of the Whig families.
In another aspect it was a question of the coherency of
Cabinets and the authority of the House of Commons.
Carteret ignored the Cabinet, where he was outvoted by
four to one, and he practically renounced the Cabinet
system. A wit said of him that he would do better if he
studied Parliament more and Demosthenes less. These,
and his rash and unsound schemes in foreign policy,
apart from all old memories, were good grounds why
Walpole should never lend him the weight of his
support.

Walpole throughout this difficult time behaved like
a man of honour and a faithful public servant. "The
king," says Horace Walpole, "is not less obliged to Lord
Orford for the defence of his crown, now he is out of
place, than when he was in the administration. His zeal,
his courage, his attention, are indefatigable and incon-

ceivable. He regards his own life no more than when it
was most his duty to expose it, and fears for everything
but that." [1]   When the king and Carteret were sorely
pressed by the thunders of Pitt and Chesterfield against
the Hanoverian troops, as well as by the tricks and vacil-
lations of the Pelhams, it was Walpole who by the
energy of his persuasion induced his friends to support the
royal measures.   He had sat for two years in the House
of Lords without addressing them, but on an occasion
(February 1744) when he thought they were neglecting
certain information laid before them about the Pretender,
he suddenly rose and made one of his finest and most
animated speeches. [2] He had not quailed before ministers
when they were intriguing and hunting him out of power,
and he braved unpopularity now, that they might use
their power for the public good.   The same men were
playing the same game against Carteret, as Carteret and
they together had played against him.   If any one asks
how Walpole's position had been more defensible towards
his colleagues in the old Cabinet, than Carteret's was
now, the answer is simple ; Walpole had a majority in
the House of Commons, and when he lost his majority,
he gave up his post.   Carteret never had a majority, he
had not even a party.   The Duke of Newcastle, said
the king, is grown as jealous of Lord Granville (Carteret's new title) as he was of Lord Orford, and wants
to be first minister himself.   Pelham was jealous both
of Granville and of his own brother, the duke.   At last
the struggle in the Cabinet grew too fierce to be
prolonged, and the Pelham faction informed the king,

[1] H. W. to Mann, 16th February 1744, i. 290.
[2] Coxe. ch. 62, iv. 333.

just as Godolphin and Marlborough had informed Queen Anne in the case of Harley in 1708, that he must make his choice. The king in his distress sent for Walpole, who was then at Houghton, suffering miseries from stone. This move was almost certainly suggested by Lord Granville,—strange illustration of the irony of politics, for he was the man who had made the motion only three years before, that Walpole should be removed from the king's counsels for ever. Walpole discouraged reliance on Granville, as he had systematically done in the days of Queen Caroline, and sent messages to urge the king to abide by the wishes of the majority in the Cabinet. After an excruciating journey he found himself at Arlington Street. All the politicians flocked to his house, and thought he must speedily be minister again.

The political battle was settled, as Walpole would have had it settled, against Granville. The Pelham interest, aided by the influence of Walpole, was preponderant in the House of Commons, and this was now the decisive consideration. The boroughmongers had forced the king to give up Walpole, and now they forced him to give up Granville. They patched up a coalition with the patriots, humoured Pitt and eventually overcame the king's reluctance to admit him to office, and formed that Broad-Bottomed administration from which every national blessing was fondly expected. Before many months had elapsed an insurrection broke out in the royal closet. The ministers tried to coerce the king by bringing seals, staves, keys, and commissions, and resigning in a body. Granville and Bath attempted to form an administration (March 1746). It lasted, as the wits said, forty-eight hours, seven minutes, and eleven seconds. All went swimmingly, until they found they had forgotten one little point, and that was to secure a majority in either House of Parliament. The old band returned in triumph. Granville laughed and drank, owned it was mad, but would do it again to-morrow. He was even daring and senseless enough to advise the king to go down to Westminster, and remonstrate from the throne with Lords and Commons assembled, against the usage that he had received. These were the men who had led the opposition to the great administration of Walpole.

To him the drama, in which he had long played a part so staunch, so manly, and so serviceable to his country and to Europe, was no longer an object of concern. He subjected himself to extraordinary and terrible treatment for his cruel malady, bore its torments with fortitude, retained his clearness of judgment to the end, and at length with little pain expired on March 18, 1745. His remains were conveyed from Arlington Street to Houghton, where they rest, like those of Edmund Burke at Beaconsfield, without commemorative monument or name.

THE END

C52066